I Was Broke. Now I'm Not.

How My Family Won With Money

JOSEPH SANGL

NIN Publishing

Printed in the United States of America by Signature Book Printing, www.sbpbooks.com

Cover design by Ken Wilson – www.avclub.us

Library of Congress Control Number: 2014916512

Sangl, Joseph

ISBN: 978-0-692-29341-6

Second Edition

To my bride, Jenn

You are THE REASON
we are winning with money today!

Table of Contents

FOREWORD

Joe Sangl is an absolute freak — which is exactly why you should not just read, but devour this book.

As a pastor I have seen hundreds of people walk around carrying regret with them. What kind of regret? Well, there's relational regret – and then there's vocational regret – but the one that usually isn't mentioned but is probably most common is FINANCIAL regret. I know way too many people who are in debt up to their eyeballs and currently see no light at the end of the tunnel – thus leaving them feeling hopeless.

But there is hope! If you are in a financial hole you CAN get out of it … and … if you are just beginning your financial journey in life what you are about to read can save you from making dumb money decisions that could haunt you for years and prevent you from doing exactly what God has designed you to do.

I personally believe that God has a unique plan and purpose for everyone on this big ball of dirt we call earth. However, I have seen people that, because of intense financial bondage, have to delay what they know He has called them to do because "they can not afford to make that move." That is tragic!

Let me be very clear about something – what you will read in the pages that follow is NOT "how to get rich in a month" type of thing. AND – by reading this you will not discover some obscure verse in the Bible that, upon "claiming" it you will have something to force God to bless you with.

What Joe has written about here is how the "average" person who makes an "average" salary can live an "above average" life. I am sick and tired of people who say that if they just made more money then they could get

i

out of the financial prison they are in – that is BULL! You can begin your journey to freedom today, but remember, financial freedom takes work.

Which is exactly why many people never achieve it! I have met WAY too many Christians who simply want God to pay off all their financial debt – which is unfair because He's not the one who racked up the credit cards. God will help us get out of debt – but we have to be the ones who apply the wisdom He provides.

Let me be honest. This is not a very comforting book when you first read it. In fact, I sort of had a sick feeling in my stomach because of some steps I discovered that I needed to take. BUT – I can promise that if you read and apply what has been written here then you will eliminate financial regret from your life.

On a personal note – I have watched Joe and his lovely bride walk through this journey. I have listened to him yell at the television when credit card commercials come on. I have seen him pay cash for just about everything he purchases. In other words, he is smoking what he is selling. This book is not the words of some ghost writer or some guy that has an abstract theory, but rather a guy who has been buried in financial regret, came out of it and wants to help others do the same.

– Perry Noble

Perry Noble is the founding pastor of NewSpring Church in Anderson, SC – www.newspring.cc

PREFACE

"If you had one million dollars, what would you do?" my friend asked me during lunch one day. I paused mid-bite of some delicious refried beans and rice to consider his question. For the first time in my life, I really thought about the real point of the question: "What have you been put on this earth to do?"

I had no idea the influence this question would come to have on my life.

The year was 1999 and I was having lunch with Tim, a fellow engineer, at a restaurant in Clemson, South Carolina. It was a typical ordinary day. Just lunch. Just friendly conversation. Just time for a break from work. And time for a life-changing question.

"If you had one million dollars, what would you do?" What a question! I thought about it, but I could not give Tim an answer. I was positive that if I had a million dollars, I *would not* be doing what I was doing then. But I had no clue regarding what I would do.

"If you had one million dollars, what would you do?" This question really messed me up. I thought about it the rest of the day. That evening, I told my wife, Jenn, about the conversation with Tim. I told her of my struggle to provide a good answer to his question.

"What?" Jenn exclaimed. "You couldn't even think of some vacations we could take?"

"That's not the point of the question," I replied. "The point of the question is NOT what temporary things you would do. The point is what would you do for your life's work? What have you been put on this earth to do?"

From that very day, I began to search for exactly what I have been put on this earth to do. That one thing I have been created to do. That one thing that wells up a passion in me like no other. That one thing that makes me wake up every single day and say, "Yes!!! I get to go to work!!!"

This book is a fulfillment of that search. It is the very thing I have been put on this earth to do. My life's passion statement is "to help people accomplish far more than they ever thought possible." And it is my hope to help you accomplish far more than you ever thought possible with your personal finances.

Helping others with their personal finances is my life's work. In this book, I have put together information I believe is foundational to financial success.

Jenn and I have applied these principles and tools to our lives and achieved financial freedom. If you apply the principles and tools taught in this book, you will also be able to win financially.

You can do this!

1 Introduction

I met Jenn at college. It was my first weekend as a freshman at Purdue University in West Lafayette, Indiana. I was committed to keeping my education first and foremost in my life. However, after meeting Jenn I tossed aside my educational focus.

Even without a laser-like focus on my education, I managed to earn a Bachelor of Science Degree in Mechanical Engineering, and I even did it in four years. I learned a lot about heat and mass transfer, thermodynamics, statics, and dynamics. I also learned about ESPN, friendships, other cultures, and living without accountability to anyone. I learned how to earn money, but I did not learn *anything* about how to manage it.

Digging a financial hole …

How did I pay for college? Loans, of course. I had borrowed money from my father for the first two years. For the final two years, my friend Sallie Mae took care of me with student loans. I managed to pay cash for about one semester's tuition and all of my books by working during the summers, but Sallie Mae Student Loan Company funded the rest.

After four years of vacation … uh, I mean, college, I completed my engineering degree. I started my first full-time engineering job the day after I graduated.

Now, work ethic has never been a problem for me. But money management? Well, that is another story!

I was earning a great salary as a beginning engineer, but what do you think I did with the money I earned? That's right! I spent all of it – plus some more.

Jenn had decided to obtain some additional classes which required her to attend Purdue for one additional year. We were engaged during that year and our wedding date was set for about a month after her graduation.

I had been working for a year, and was fully aware that Jenn's car situation needed to be addressed. Her vehicle had been sitting, broken down and abandoned in a Purdue residence hall parking lot for six months. This was a clear sign it needed to be replaced.

I thought it would be really awesome to buy her a brand new car for her graduation gift. So that is exactly what I did. I had no savings, so I purchased a new car with 105% financing. I even financed the sales tax! I am quite sure I paid full retail price (and then some) for that car. I am also certain I made that car salesman's quota for the entire quarter, maybe even his year!

It was a great moment to watch Jenn's reaction as she unwrapped her graduation presents. I remember her removing each of her graduation gifts from the box I had given her and discovering a Purdue University license plate holder at the bottom. I then reached out and handed her the keys to her new car. It was an amazing moment. She was pumped! I was fired up too, but I also knew how much car debt we had just acquired.

A few weeks later, we were married! Off we went to Jamaica for our honeymoon with much of it financed with debt. We needed appliances for our unfurnished apartment, so we purchased all of them with credit. I wanted a truck, so I bought a used one from my father with no money down.

I had purchased quite a few things on credit cards during college and my spending habits did not change after graduation. I could always pay the monthly payments, but somehow the debt continued accumulating on the accounts. Advanta – my first credit card. The GM Card – another card. MBNA, Capital One, American Express, and the list goes on.

Here is a summary of all of the debt we (mostly me!) brought into our brand new marriage:

- Credit Cards
- New Car
- Used Truck
- Appliances
- Dad's College Loans (Mine)
- Sallie Mae Student Loans (Mine)
- Sallie Mae Student Loans (Hers)

They say the number one thing married couples fight about is money, so this is just what our new marriage needed – a pile of debt to manage.

We were horrible at prioritizing short-term savings. We spent everything we brought home, plus some more. How did we spend more than we brought home? Debt! We piled up even more debt on our credit cards.

Our money management techniques were unique and strange. I had arranged with our payroll service to have $200 automatically deducted from every single paycheck and deposited into a savings account. It seemed like a great way to ensure we saved money. On payday, however, I would immediately transfer the $200 back into the checking account and spend it. We needed it to pay our bills.

Each time I was paid, we experienced an interesting balancing act because we would have to figure out which paycheck was going to pay each of our bills. If there was an unplanned expense like a car repair, it was a financial disaster! We would scramble to pay as many bills as we could and then use credit cards to pick up the rest.

Nine months after we were married, I accepted a job transfer that required a move from our home in Indiana to Anderson, South Carolina. This move meant we were now living in a place where we literally knew no one. It was a great time of learning about each other and strengthening our commitment to our marriage. I highly recommend that couples do this at least once in their life! However, in keeping with our tradition, it was also time to acquire more debt. We realized The American Dream by purchasing our first home.

By some miracle, we managed to scrape together a five-percent down payment and qualify for a conventional mortgage for our first house. Our family of debts now had a new member, but this one was different than the others – it was six figures. Yikes!

We chose not to change our spending behavior so debts continued to build. Our checking and savings account balances hovered around an average of $4.13. "At least the balance is a *positive* $4.13," I would say to myself.

Then the unbelievable and awesome tremendous news came that a baby was on the way! This baby was a miracle because Jenn had experienced ovarian tumors when she was a teenager, and doctors were unsure if she would be able to have children. We were so excited, but I also knew this news was going to impact the family's finances because it was Jenn's dream to be a stay-at-home mom. While Jenn had been working as a teacher, I had complained that educators were not paid enough (I still hold this view!). Now, faced with the loss of her paycheck, I began to hold the view that teachers were paid huge amounts of money!

Our beautiful daughter showed up on a wonderful South Carolina November morning. It is a day I will never forget. I cried like a baby. I was so proud. I was so moved by God's creation. I was so moved by His faithfulness to Jenn and me. I truly understood for the first time what "my Father's love" really means. It is unbreakable and unshakable. It is forever.

Well, Jenn came home with the baby and began telling others that she had retired from teaching. She said it with a sly smile, but I didn't think it was funny! We began the challenge of operating our household on just my income. While we adjusted our spending some, we continued to utilize credit cards to fill in the gaps.

After three years in Anderson, I accepted a job transfer to a manufacturing facility near Columbia, South Carolina. We sold our house in Anderson and used a good portion of the equity to help pay off some credit card debt.

It was a tough move. Jenn and I had made a lot of great friendships in Anderson and had assisted with starting a new church that was awesome and growing. Our hearts remained back in Anderson while we lived two hours away in Columbia.

After living in Columbia for a year, we decided to move back to our home state of Indiana to live closer to our families. This required a change of employers, so I embarked on a job search. I found a great job in northern Indiana, and we moved on December 1, 2002.

Time to change spending behavior ...

On December 2, 2002, our new hometown in northern Indiana provided a rude weather greeting. It was eight degrees outside with eight inches of snow on the ground. Snow was not foreign to us, but we had been living in South Carolina for the past four-and-a-half years. It was a shock to experience this weather again! Our family took up temporary residence in an extended stay hotel room while we embarked on the search for a new home.

We had known we were going to be changing employers for about six months. It was no surprise that we were going to be moving a long distance. Do you think we financially prepared for the move? No way!

We had no clue when I was going to be paid by my new employer, and it was Christmas season. We began loading up the credit cards again. We felt the need to purchase stuff for our child and each other, so out came the credit card. We paid for our groceries with the credit card. We paid for regular living expenses with a credit card. It was not good.

This marked the third time in our life where we found ourselves loading up the credit cards. We had taken multiple large tax refunds and paid credit card debt down before, yet here we were again, running the balance up. Just writing about it makes my blood pressure go up and my face flush red. I was extremely unhappy about it and felt great discouragement.

Thoughts raced through my head. Thoughts like: "How is this possible?" and "Why is this happening again?" and "This should not be happening!" and "This is embarrassing!" and "This has GOT to change!" and "How do I make this stop?" and "Who can I talk to that can help me with this?" and "I am a three-time loser with credit cards!"

Ever had any of these thoughts? It was in this moment that Jenn and I experienced what I call an "**I Have Had Enough Moment**" (an IHHE Moment). We came up with a plan to fix the financial mess. We chopped up the credit cards. We refused to sign up for any more debt – with the one exception of a home mortgage.

We began to plan our spending every single month before the month began. Some might call it budgeting, but I would call it "telling your money what to do instead of having your money tell you what to do."

In fourteen short months, we became debt-free except for our house. Our debt freedom allowed us to build up a savings account balance that we never thought was possible.

We no longer have ridiculous stress related to our finances. We have financial freedom. Our marriage has grown stronger. We are committed to always work together on our spending plans. It is possible to dream of the future because we are not stuck in the proverbial hamster wheel spinning away and getting nowhere.

I have been able to leave corporate America and pursue my life's passion of "helping people accomplish far more than they ever thought possible!" We were even able to negotiate a massive pay cut to take a dream job and *smile* about it because our money was under control.

We are able to teach our children how to manage money well. There is money in their college funds. Our oldest daughter starting saving for her first car when she was only four years old!

We have been able to give more money away than we ever dreamed. We are able to give the tithe and more to our church. Our beloved alma mater, Purdue University, benefits from our giving. We are able to support missionaries and other causes we deeply believe in.

There is money available in case of an emergency. Anytime something breaks like an appliance or car, we just have an appliance or car problem. We don't have an appliance problem and an accompanying money problem. We don't have a car problem and a "How on earth am I supposed to pay for this?" problem. Our retirement savings account is growing nicely. Retirement will be possible some day without relying on Social Security.

In this book I will share the details of the tools and tips we applied to accomplish financial freedom. If it were possible, I would jump out from this book and encourage you by saying, "Stick with this book. Read it. Apply this stuff. You can do this!"

I believe every single person who reads this book can apply these principles and take their finances to the next level. I believe you can become debt-free including your house and give more than you have ever given, save more than you have ever saved, and spend more than you have ever spent! I call this a *fully funded life*, and I believe you can do it!

You can accomplish far more than you ever thought possible! When you do, I hope you will pay it forward by helping someone else achieve financial freedom. By the way, in case you missed it, I believe in you!

You can do this!

2 The Catalyst For Change

It had happened again. The bills were due, it was Christmastime, and we had no extra money. We had enough money to pay bills or buy Christmas gifts, but not both.

"How on earth have we arrived at this point again?!!!" I thought to myself as I was paying the bills for the month. It was more than a little embarrassing to discuss the matter with Jenn because this was not the first time I had to approach her about this same issue.

"Jenn," I said miserably. "We do not have enough money to pay the bills and buy Christmas gifts."

"In fact," I continued, "I do not know when my new job will pay me, so we need to start putting all of our expenses on the credit card to ensure we do not run out of money."

What a horrible discussion that was. Here I was, an engineer making an excellent salary, and we had no money.

"How could this be?" I wondered out loud.

"How could this be?" Jenn asked.

What did we do? We used the credit card for the entire month of December. This was the same credit card we had already paid off twice before. We had used multiple large tax returns to pay down and pay off the credit cards. Yet, somehow, here we were again, out of money and running up the credit cards.

Something about the way we were managing money was broken. Something was wrong. It had to change.

"What should we do?" I thought.

"What can I do differently?" I prayed.

Let me introduce you to ...

As I thought about what we could do differently, my mind drifted to a conversation I had a year earlier with my brother, Mike. As I recalled the phone conversation, I smiled because the conversation had happened while I was living in Columbia, South Carolina. I had been choosing our Christmas tree at Lowe's in 70°F weather, wearing shorts and a short-sleeve shirt. While this might not seem significant for my Southern friends, this was a major event for a farm boy from Indiana. In Indiana there are approximately four months of frost-free weather, and December is NOT one of them!

While talking to Mike, he told me about this personal finance class he was taking. He rambled on and on about this class called *Financial Peace University*. It was put together by some guy named Dave Ramsey.

"Have you heard of him?" he asked me.

"No, I don't think I have," I responded distractedly as I picked out the Christmas tree.

"You should look the class up," Mike said. "His name is Dave Ramsey."

"Okay," I had replied half-heartedly, ending the phone call.

Now, here I was a year later, suddenly very interested in what my brother had said. I could not remember the name of the guy teaching the class, but with a quick phone call to Mike, I was reminded that the guy's name was Dave Ramsey and the class was named *Financial Peace University*.

The day we made the decision …

I went the next day to a bookstore and purchased Dave's book, *Financial Peace, Revisited*. I read the entire book that night.

"You need to read this book immediately," I told Jenn as I handed it to her. She did.

Once she had completed the book, we discussed what we had read and determined the key financial steps we should take. We were sick of living paycheck-to-paycheck. We were sick of not ever having any money in our savings account. What we had been doing was not working. We had to make a change.

Making it happen …

That very evening, Jenn and I pulled out all of our credit cards and cut them up. I called the credit card company and despite their strong persuasive arguments, I had the account shut down.

With the action of cutting up the credit cards, we were really declaring *together* that we were finished with debt. We were making a proclamation that from that day forward, we were going to manage our financial resources differently. It was a landmark moment in the lives of Joseph and Jennifer Sangl. Quite frankly, it was a defining moment for our entire family.

Seven months later, we had a balanced budget that was written down on paper. Fourteen months later, we were debt-free except for our house. In just five additional months, we had fully funded our emergency fund with three month's expenses. In a total of twenty-six months, we were able to save enough for our car replacement fund.

In the meantime, we were able to start funding our first daughter's 529 college fund. Once the replacement car fund was completed, we were able to double the monthly contribution to her college fund!

Upon completion of the car fund, we began to attack the house debt. I took a blueprint schematic of the house plan and scanned it in to my computer. I then outlined the outside walls of our house and inserted a huge quantity of small squares into the house drawing. I counted the number of squares and divided them into the purchase price of the house. Every little square equaled $102.92 in principal. Every time we paid off $102.92 in principal, we got to color-in a square! I called this chart "The Sangl Family Home Pay-off Spectacular."

I became a maniac. I wanted out of debt and was committed to do whatever it took to accomplish our goal!

Do you want to truly understand how much of your home you own? Prepare a visual chart like this for your own home. You will clearly understand just how much debt you really have.

When we started out, we did not own much of our home at all. I began coloring in the squares where our bathroom was located. "A man needs to at least know he owns his throne!" I told Jenn with a smirk.

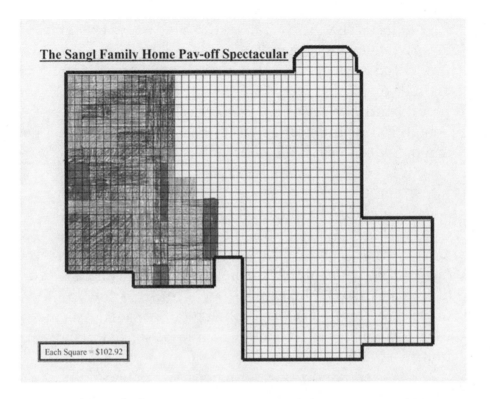

The Sangl Family Home Pay-off Spectacular

Each Square = $102.92

Commitment is tested ...

While we were diligently working to eliminate our debt, Jenn received bad medical news. During vacation in San Diego, she had felt some serious stomach pains. A visit to the doctor revealed a mass. A major surgery was performed and a large ovarian tumor was removed.

We were grateful to receive the news of a benign tumor, but the surgery resulted in large medical bills. We had good health insurance, but we were still responsible for a large deductible. While the bills took their four month journey through the insurance payment process, we were able to absorb the deductible as part of our monthly budget plans and pay the bills as they arrived. Now, it did delay our debt pay-off plans, but because we no longer had car payments, student loan payments, NO

PAYMENTS EXCEPT THE HOUSE, we were able to absorb this major expense.

Ten months later, the tumors returned resulting in another major surgery. We received another benign tumor report, and we were so thankful. It was not, however, benign to our finances as large medical bills appeared yet again. Once again, we were able to absorb the major expense.

THIS IS WHY I DO NOT ACCEPT EXCUSES!

If my family could weather the storms our finances have faced, you can too! I believe most financial success or failure is directly related to one's attitude toward their debts. We stopped being broke emotionally and mentally long before our bank account started showing improvement.

As Jenn and I began to focus our financial attention on eliminating our home mortgage debt, we also began turning our thoughts toward the church we had helped start while living in Anderson, South Carolina – NewSpring Church. While I was experiencing some success in corporate America, there was a tug on my heart to help others experience the financial freedom I had achieved.

After many months of prayer, thoughts, and conversations, I resigned from my job and accepted the role as Pastor of Financial Planning and Coaching at NewSpring Church. In this role, I was able to focus on helping fund the vision of the church and begin mentoring and coaching families with the tools I had been able to use to achieve financial freedom.

It was incredible to be able to serve on pastoral staff, but it also required a financial sacrifice. In fact, I agreed to nearly a fifty-percent pay cut. I did not expect nor require the church to pay what corporate America was paying me. Because Jenn and I had eliminated all of our non-house debt, we were able to accept far less income and continue to thrive!

I began teaching personal finance classes at NewSpring Church, and the response was amazing. In the first year in my new role, I was able to provide one-on-one financial coaching to 650 people. The response to our live group training events was also incredible. We had 360 people show up at our first ever Financial Learning Experience – the two-hour live event I now teach around the world.

In 2008 the world economy began to descend into a tremendous recession, and I began receiving phone calls from other churches and businesses asking me to come help their congregations and team members. At this same time, I was completing the writing phase of the first edition of this book, *I Was Broke. Now I'm Not.*

Because we were unknown to the book publishing world, we had to make a decision between self-publishing the book or pursuing a publishing agreement. Again, Dave Ramsey spoke great wisdom to me. I was invited to meet him during one of his daily broadcasts, and I asked him what I should do. He challenged me to self-publish the book saying, "Do print it, and do sell it. It's worth it, man!"

Because we were debt-free, it was possible for us to save the money necessary to pay for this book to be self-published. People responded to this message of hope by purchasing thousands of copies within a few months. It became clear that the need for this teaching was great. Over the course of the next year, we took steps to register I Was Broke. Now I'm Not., LLC as a business.

Due to the number of speaking requests, it was becoming difficult to fulfill my duties as a pastor. A decision had to be made. I needed to either stay in my current role as a pastor or take the plunge into launching I Was Broke. Now I'm Not., LLC (IWBNIN).

It was a major life-altering decision. One thing I've learned over my life is that large financial and life decisions always present tremendous life challenges. This one was no different.

You see, Jenn and I both desired to have more than one child, but it was not possible due to the multiple surgeries she had endured. If we wanted more children, the doctors advised, we would need to attempt IVF (In Vitro Fertilization). After much time and consideration, we made the decision to pursue it. As anyone who has been through this process can attest, IVF is not cheap, and it is a very emotional process. As we were considering launching IWBNIN, the time was right to pursue having another child as our only child, Melea, was already nine years old.

Our IVF attempt in January 2009 was unsuccessful. While this was not the outcome we had prayed for, it did provide a sense of closure for us. We made the decision to launch IWBNIN and on June 1, 2009, I stepped into the world of small business ownership.

This new business was now responsible for our financial health – income and benefits. When obtaining health insurance, my insurance agent informed me that maternity insurance was a supplemental and optional insurance. He also told me the maternity insurance would only cover 20-percent of the costs of a pregnancy and delivery in the first year, 40-percent in the next, and 60-percent in the third year. Only after having the policy for four years would it begin to cover 100-percent of the cost – after a massive deductible, of course.

Since we had not been able to have children for more than nine years and had unsuccessfully attempted IVF, I opted out of the maternity insurance. You know what happened next, right? That's right. On June 16, 2009, just sixteen days after embarking upon our small business ownership journey, we received the astounding news that a baby was on the way! It was an amazing, emotional, shocking, and frightening moment – all at the same time. While we were thrilled with the news, we also knew insurance would not be paying anything for this child.

For the first two months, IWBNIN had no customers. None. We had prepared for the launch of this business by cutting expenses and saving money. However, no business can succeed without sales! Our first work was scheduled for late August. Just a few days before traveling to meet with our first client, I received a late night email canceling the meeting. They said they did not have money to pay us.

I began thinking about writing a sequel to this book called, *I Was Broke. Then I Wasn't. Now I Am Again.* Passion, however, will make you stick with a dream longer than you probably should. I called the client and told them I would still come help them despite not having the money to pay us. After all, it *was my calling* to help people who are struggling financially! We were able to serve this client and helped them a great deal. They were so impacted that they ended up being able to pay us!

During our first year of IWBNIN, we made so little money that we qualified for low-income benefits. We were willing, however, to sacrifice income to see the dream come to life.

In February 2010, we welcomed our son, Keaton, into our lives. We were blessed to pay cash for his hospital bills.

Ever since those challenging moments in 2009, Jenn and I have reaped the benefits of having a financial plan and a budget. We've been able to fund dreams we never thought were possible. One dream was to live on a farm. Since I had grown up in the cornfields of Indiana, it had always been my dream to own acreage so my children could run free like I did as a child. Shortly after our son arrived, we were blessed to be able to purchase a farm.

In 2011, through a series of miracles, I was even able to purchase a company! I bought INJOY Stewardship Solutions, an organization founded by noted leadership guru, Dr. John C. Maxwell. This organization helps churches raise money to build facilities, pay off debt, and fund major ministry initiatives.

In January 2013, my family made the final payment on our home mortgage and experienced the joy of seeing a Wells Fargo mortgage statement that contained the words "Paid In Full."

The good news did not stop there. In that very same month, we discovered that another child was on the way! Later that year, we welcomed another baby girl, Megan, into our home.

You can do this!

I do not share my journey with you to impress you. I share it because *it is my real journey* and none of it would have been possible without making the decision to apply the tools and principles contained within this book.

You might be reading this and believe this sort of financial success is not possible for you. I am here to tell you IT IS POSSIBLE! You can do this!

This was accomplished because Jenn and I decided *together* that what we had been doing was unacceptable. It was possible because Jenn and I decided *together* that we were not effectively managing the resources God had provided us. This happened because Jenn and I decided *together* to do something about it. We committed *together* to change *our* behavior.

Beyond our decision and newfound commitment, we actually *did something different.* As a result, our lives will NEVER be the same.

Jenn and I have learned a lot about our finances as we have journeyed through this together, but even more, we have learned a lot about each other. We have a better marriage because we work together on our finances.

Do you feel clueless about your finances? Do you want to learn how to achieve financial freedom? Are you tired of living paycheck-to-paycheck? Are you sick of fighting about money with your spouse? Have you been burned by debt? Are you looking for a way out? Do you want to be able to tell a story about how your life has dramatically changed?

The Critical Question

Have you reached a point where you are willing to make a major change to the way you manage your money? If so, this book has been written for you. It is time for YOU to achieve your own story of financial freedom.

You can do this!

3 There Must Be A Plan!

You must have a plan for your life in order to win with money. This is because your life decisions ultimately drive your financial decisions.

Ask any person who runs a business, and they will tell you how crucial planning is to achieving their business goals. Let's look at some common examples of planning.

Football Games

Here in South Carolina, we have two universities that have a huge rivalry. These two teams are Clemson University and the University of South Carolina. It is an intense rivalry no matter how you look at it, but it becomes white-hot burning craziness when you put these two schools together on a football field.

Do you think these two schools show up on game day and only then begin thinking about what they are going to do on the field? NOT A CHANCE!

From the day of last year's game, they begin preparing a plan for next year's match-up. They know which players are graduating. They know the players who will still be there. They plan accordingly.

In fact, there are multiple plans being prepared. There are ten different coaches on the roster of the Clemson Tigers football team. They have a head coach, offensive coordinator, running backs coach, offensive line coach, wide receivers coach, tight ends coach, defensive coordinator, defensive line coach, linebackers coach, and a defensive ends coach. These are just the coaches needed to prepare the team for the game.

From the day of the last rivalry game to the day of next year's game, they are PLANNING. All of this effort for one single game one day each year – not to mention the other ten or eleven games on each team's schedule.

Building a House

Would you build a house without a detailed set of plans? As the son of a homebuilder, I know that pages and pages of plans are painstakingly prepared before the first hole is dug and the first nail is hammered. There are plans outlining the elevations of the finished house, foundation placement, framing, HVAC, plumbing, and electrical.

It would be crazy to spend money constructing a new home without first putting together a plan.

Surgery

What if your knee required surgery? Suppose you met with the surgeon and he said, "I'm not really sure what I am going to do. I think I am just going to start cutting on you and see whether or not we can fix this. I hope it works out. By the way, you're my first patient."

Would you hang around? Not a chance! If a doctor said this to me, I'm confident a vapor trail would be formed by the speed in which I departed the medical center.

I want the surgeon to be trained, certain, and confident. Even more, I want him to know for sure what he is going to do should an unexpected event take place during the surgery. The surgeon must have a detailed plan!

Wedding

Ever attended an unplanned wedding? Enough said!

War

Would a military officer go to war without a plan? Deciding to finally prepare a plan in the midst of bombs, gunfire, and tanks cruising in toward the troops would be catastrophic.

Consider each of these examples:

- If football teams plan all year for one game
- If you would demand detailed house plans before constructing a new home
- If you would demand your surgeon have a plan for your knee surgery
- If you would plan a wedding before saying the life changing words, "I do."
- If a military officer would develop a battle plan before making war

If we have countless examples proving the importance of planning, why on earth would you not plan your finances? It is crazy to spend money without having a plan for your finances. Your financial condition literally dictates your very ability to accomplish your God-given hopes and dreams!

Most young people today will earn more than $2,000,000 over their lifetime. Which will better help them maximize their income: Preparing a detailed financial plan or not having one? To prosper, money must be planned. Have I sufficiently proven the need for a financial plan?

Ultimately, there are three things necessary for you to plan your finances effectively.

1. A clear understanding of WHY you want to achieve financial freedom
2. A monthly written plan for your spending (yes – a budget – it's EZ™!)
3. A clear financial path to follow

The remainder of this book is focused on helping you implement all three items so you can live a fully funded life.

You can do this!

4 The IWBNIN Ladder

As I climbed out of my financial mess, I became so fired up that I began teaching other people to implement the same principles I was following. I would meet with people at work, in their homes, and at our church to help them walk through the financial challenges they were facing.

We would work together to document their plans, hopes, and dreams and then move toward preparing a budget to support their key goals. Our next step would focus on addressing their debts. Then I would bring up the topics of insurance and investing. It quickly became a confusing spiral of topics resulting in a key question: "Which item should I focus on first?" The need for a financial roadmap became very apparent.

For many years, I worked to define the steps I took to gain control of my money and position myself to prosper. This effort has resulted in a financial tool called the I Was Broke. Now I'm Not. Ladder – *9 Rungs To A Fully Funded Life*. This is a guide millions of people have followed to gain control of their money and achieve their dreams. I know it can help you do the same.

A Fully Funded Life

It is important to understand what is meant by a "fully funded life." I define this as the ability to do exactly what you have been put on earth to do – regardless of the cost or income potential. One person might have dreams that cost $50 thousand while another has plans costing more than $1 million. Regardless of the cost of your dreams, it is my passion to help you accomplish them so you can look back over your life and say, "I lived a fully funded life."

Money Has Rules

Just like any game, money has rules. Rules like "spend less than you make" and "save money for a rainy day." If you follow the rules, you will make sustainable financial progress. If you choose to skip some rules, you may see improvements, but it could leave you exposed to financial harm later in your money journey. The IWBNIN Ladder will help ensure you take steps in an order that will make your goals achievable.

The I Was Broke. Now I'm Not. Ladder
Rung #1 *Set goals*

Most people allow their current financial position to dictate their dreams. It should be the other way around! If most people were to allow their current financial position to drive their dreams, they wouldn't be allowed to dream. Alas, most people find themselves with very little money, and believe they can't pursue their dreams. "I just don't want to end up disappointed again," they tell me.

Don't allow this to happen to you! In Dr. John C. Maxwell's great book, *Put Your Dream To The Test*, he shares that dreaming is awesome because, in the beginning, dreams are *free*.

The late great motivator, Zig Ziglar, shared his thoughts regarding the importance of setting goals this way, "If you aim at nothing, you will hit every time."

Your goals will help you stick with the financial decisions necessary to climb up the ladder, even when everything and everyone is telling you to just let it go.

Rung #2 *Save money – Start with one month of expenses*

Saved money allows you to build something called financial margin. Margin is an alternative way to communicate "space." Remember when the English teacher ruined your life by announcing that you must hand write a two page composition? She would say, "Be sure to avoid writing in the *margins*." In other words, it was important to maintain appropriate spacing.

The same is true for your finances. Financial margin creates space in your life. It allows you to breathe. A life event such as a car repair, emergency trip out of town, appliance failure, or unexpected school fundraiser can arise without trashing your finances.

Saving one month of expenses allows you to manage your finances with a monthly budget, even if you are paid at some other frequency (like weekly or every two weeks). As you will soon see in the budgeting chapters, preparing a monthly budget is substantially easier than planning every paycheck.

Rung #3 *Invest enough to capture full company match (or $100/month – whichever is greater)*

According to a recent report by FINRA (an organization focused on protecting American investors), 29.4% of retirement plan participants do not contribute enough to receive their full employer match. This rate increases to 43% for younger workers with ages between 20 and 29. These workers are missing out on free money!

Be certain you are receiving the full matching contribution from your employer. If you do not have an employer provided retirement savings plan, open your own account and contribute at least $100 each month. This is important because investing early and often allows you to capture the tremendous power of compound interest and will play a huge role in funding the goals you have written down when climbing Rung #1.

Investing is a confusing topic for many people. If you are one of them, you will be glad to know this book contains an entire chapter focused on investing.

Rung #4 *Eliminate all non-house, non-business debt*

Once you have climbed Rungs #1 through #3, it is finally time to tackle debt. Some common debts eliminated in Rung #4 include vehicle loans, student loans, credit card balances, furniture purchases, debt consolidation loans, signature loans, and debts owed to friends and family.

The average family can eliminate their non-house, non-business debt in three years or less. Achievement of this rung requires focused diligence, but the reward is amazing.

When this rung is achieved, a person's cost of living drops substantially – usually somewhere around fifteen percent! This provides more margin in the monthly budget which, in turn, allows an individual to build additional savings and investments to fund Rung #1 goals.

Rung #5 *Build savings to a minimum of three months of expenses*

Achievement of Rung #4 frees up all of the payments being sent to lenders. With this money now available for saving, the average person can accomplish Rung #5 in less than a year.

Consider the feeling of having at least three months of expenses in the bank – just for emergencies and opportunities. If you have achieved this before, you know how great it feels. If not, join me on the IWBNIN ladder and begin climbing. You will be at Rung #5 before you know it!

Rung #6 *Place 15% of gross income into tax-advantaged investments*

Now that you have eliminated your non-house, non-business debt and built a large emergency savings balance, you can focus on funding the larger goals you established in Rung #1. This is accomplished by increasing your investments to 15% of your gross income – your income before taxes and deductions.

Since you have already initiated your investments during Rung #3, this rung only requires a decision on where to invest your money. My book, *Oxen: The Key To An Abundant Harvest*, focuses heavily on this topic. We will also spend time on this subject later on in the Investing chapter.

Rung #7 *Pay off house and business debt*

At this position on the IWBNIN Ladder, you are in exclusive territory. You have positioned yourself to accomplish huge dreams in life – dreams like "paying off the house."

While this seems like an enormous and potentially unachievable goal when beginning at Rung #1, it is not nearly as difficult once Rung #6 is achieved. Consider the progress that has been made. All other debt has been eliminated, savings accounts are full, investing is happening at a high level, and you will have tremendous financial margin in your monthly budget. This bodes well for swift mortgage elimination.

The average family starting at Rung #1 of the IWBNIN Ladder can accomplish Rung #7 within ten years of embarking upon their climb. I was able to eliminate my mortgage on my house in just 72 months – six years – from the date we purchased it. You can do this too!

Rung #8 *Place 30% of gross income into tax-advantaged investments*

Achievement of Rung #7 will free up the monthly mortgage payment. For the average family, this equals an additional 25% of their income – maybe even more. This means the investment increase from Rung #6 (15%) to this rung (30%) will be accomplished while still having additional money left over to fund your dreams!

Rung #9 *Live a great life!*

This final rung represents the end of a challenging climb. It is time to enjoy the view! It will be at this moment you will realize how well you've positioned yourself to bless others – your family, those who are in great need, and causes you want to support.

You will even discover that throughout the entire journey, you have lived a great life! A smile will appear on your face as you reflect on your climb. You will remember the time when paying for a car repair seemed impossible, yet you made it. You will reflect on the day you were thunderstruck as you realized your baby was now a teenager and college was just around the corner. Then the thought of "How in the world will we ever pay for tuition?" crossed your mind, but somehow you were able to accomplish it!

Your story will be unique, but the climb will be shared with countless others who have resolved to live a different sort of life – a *fully funded life*.

Why It's Called A Ladder – It Requires Effort

I discovered it took enormous work and focus to climb out of my financial hole. In fact, once I was out of my immediate mess and achieved financial stability, it required great diligence to remain there. Climbing a real ladder requires tremendous effort, and climbing the IWBNIN financial ladder is no different. Every movement upward to another rung is a challenge which demands focused attention and effort.

It is also very challenging, perhaps impossible, to skip a rung. Just as a person would climb a ladder "rung by rung," the IWBNIN Ladder should also be ascended in the same manner. Skipping a rung could result in a terrible fall, leaving one's finances battered and bruised. Follow the rungs in order, and you will have a successful climb.

The most common mistake made by people just beginning their financial journey is attempting to jump on the ladder at Rung #4 – completely skipping Rungs #1 through #3. This is usually because they are frustrated with their debt situation and really want to eliminate it. In their haste, they begin attacking debt without documenting their goals (Rung #1), saving money (Rung #2), or beginning to invest (Rung #3). All available money is applied to debt. Every month, they send the maximum amount possible to kill their debt.

They make excellent progress until their car breaks down and the refrigerator fails – in the same month. Because Rungs #2 and #3 were skipped, they have no savings or investments to pay for the car repair and to replace the refrigerator. In a demoralizing setback, they are forced to use debt again.

Since they chose to skip Rung #1, they don't have any written goals to remind them of why they are attempting to win with money. This can cause them to lose heart and cease their attempt to climb the ladder. Don't skip rungs, they are in a specific order for a reason!

Why It's Called A Ladder – It Changes Your Perspective

As you climb a real ladder, your perspective will change. As a deer hunter, I have discovered this truth firsthand. For most of my life, I had chosen to hunt on the ground. To maximize my chance for success, I would find a good place to hide along a well-traveled deer path and sit very quietly and hope for a deer to arrive. This worked very well for seeing deer. In fact, I've had some amazing and very close encounters with them.

There was just one problem. By the time I saw the deer, they were so close that there was usually no way for me to move into position to obtain my quarry. With my first movement, the deer would spot me and disappear in a flash.

To address this issue, I purchased a ladder stand. These are special ladders that can be positioned against trees located near the deer paths. As I climbed up the 17-foot ladder for the first time, I was astonished at the change in perspective it provided me. At ground level, I could usually see about thirty feet in front of me. However, as I climbed to the top of the ladder stand, I could see a distance of several hundred yards!

By climbing the ladder, I was able to see deer long before they could ever see me. This provided an opportunity to move into position so I was ready when the right moment came. My hunting results dramatically improved.

The same is true for your finances. As you climb the ladder, your perspective will shift. You will be able to see expenses far ahead of you and make the financial decisions necessary to prepare for them. In January, you will see the oncoming expense of Christmas. As a result, you will be able to save for Christmas every month of the entire year. Even though your car is operating beautifully, now you will anticipate the need for car repairs as well as ongoing maintenance items like replacing brakes and tires and begin saving money for them.

Even more exciting, you will also be able to see financial opportunities! You see, when I was hunting on the ground, I had no idea if there were deer anywhere near me until they were directly in front of me. However, my view from the top of the ladder revealed deer (opportunity!) moving far away from me. The same is true for your finances.

For example, when a person achieves Rung #2, they are able to eliminate a lot of daily financial stress. It allows them to take advantage of the opportunity to pay the annual cost for a health club membership and save two months of fees. It affords them the ability to increase their home insurance deductible to $1,000 instead of $500 and enjoy a $400 per year reduction in the annual insurance premium.

When Rung #5 is achieved, a family can really consider many more opportunities for their life. For instance, suppose a person desired a different job, but it paid $1,000 less per month. When living at "ground level" on the IWBNIN Ladder, they could not even consider taking the job because it would create a financial train wreck. However, when Rung #5 is achieved, they have eliminated all of their non-house, non-business debt and saved at least three months of expenses. This can allow them to take the new lower-paying position without causing any financial harm.

Do you see it? The ladder can change your perspective and allow you to see opportunities *already around you*, but can't be seen until you begin climbing.

Use the IWBNIN Ladder to help guide you through your next financial decisions. Download a personal copy of the IWBNIN Ladder at www.iwbnin.com/ladder and determine the rung you are currently standing upon. Then set goals (part of Rung #1) for the rungs still ahead of you on your financial journey.

Why It's Called A Ladder – It Requires A Solid Foundation

If you have ever attempted to climb a real ladder, you know the importance of establishing a solid foundation beneath it to provide support. My father owned and operated a home construction business for more than fifty years, and we constantly used ladders. From my earliest memories, I remember climbing them. Many times, there was a lot of loose and uneven soil around the new home we were building. As we positioned the ladder, we made sure to firm up the foundation below it – usually with concrete blocks or pieces of lumber.

This focus on establishing a firm foundation before climbing the ladder isn't too important if one only needs to climb a single rung to perform a task. As the old saying goes, "If you fall off the first rung of a 20-foot ladder, would you get hurt?" The answer is, "No, because you fell from the *first* rung."

However, if you are preparing to climb the entire ladder, you will demand a solid foundation. Without it, the ladder is subject to sudden movements which could lead to serious injury or even death.

Your climb up the IWBNIN Ladder requires a solid foundation of support. There are key financial tools and principles that will help ensure you experience a stable climb.

These key IWBNIN Ladder foundational tools and principles include:

- Goals
- Monthly budgeting
- Income
- Giving
- Saving
- Debt snowball
- No bad debt
- Insurance
- Investing
- Automation
- Partnership
- Self control
- Diligence and persistence
- Estate planning
- Coaching
- Continual learning

The remainder of this book will focus on equipping you to successfully implement these foundational principles into your own financial journey. When you put them into place and make it your habit to apply them, you will soon be living a *fully funded life*.

You can do this!

5 Why Do You Want Financial Freedom?

"What's your fuel?", a friend of mine, Mike Yoder, asked me.

"Pardon me?" I questioned.

"Why are you doing this with your finances? What's driving you?" Mike asked. "What's your fuel?"

I have thought a lot about Mike's question. Why would someone pursue financial freedom? What are the reasons a person would want freedom from debt? Why would they wait until they had enough money to pay cash for an item instead of using debt to buy it immediately?

I truly believe the answer is not "to get rich." It simply isn't the "fuel" for most people. Through our team's research, we've identified the following items as the "fuel" for becoming financially free, and I encourage you to check all the ones that apply to you.

Fuel For Becoming Financially Free

☐ Eliminating the STRESS of paycheck-to-paycheck living
☐ Allowing a spouse to work part-time or quit their job entirely to stay at home and raise the children
☐ Adopting a child
☐ Quitting a job that "just pays the bills" and pursuing work they were put on this earth to do
☐ Obtaining the ability to do what one is made to do *regardless* of the income potential
☐ Starting up a business they have always dreamed about
☐ Paying bills only one time per month
☐ Allowing a spouse to go back to college

- ☐ Sending children to college
- ☐ Providing a beautiful wedding for their daughter
- ☐ Supporting meaningful causes that one values and desires to support financially
- ☐ Quitting a job which requires a lot of overtime and taking a job earning less income but allows more family time
- ☐ Retirement
- ☐ Giving themselves a raise by managing money better
- ☐ Being able to take paid-for-in-advance vacations
- ☐ Owning a few of life's pleasures
- ☐ Eliminating money fights
- ☐ Improving marriage relationship
- ☐ Starting a non-profit organization to help others (orphanage, university, crisis pregnancy center, etc.)

All of these are awesome reasons to pursue financial freedom because they are value-focused. They reveal the values you hold highly.

Ask yourself this question: "If I keep managing money the way I am right now, will I be prevented from accomplishing my dreams?"

Perhaps you have a big dream. A dream so large you have never even revealed it to anyone for fear of their response. If you choose not to prepare a financial plan to fund it, the chance is great that you will never be able to pursue the dream. Your time will not be yours to govern. You will have to go to work every day of your life just to pay basic bills.

I no longer feel I am doing work. Instead, I am on a crusade to help people accomplish far more than they ever thought possible with their personal finances. I am championing a cause! I am sick of seeing people live paycheck-to-paycheck. I am tired of seeing people without hope. I am saddened by people who have given up on their dreams all because they exchanged them for a big lie that a $40,000 car and $10,000 TV/Sound System would make them happy. I am here to help the HOPELESS become HOPEFUL. I am here to help the DEBT-RIDDEN become DEBT-FREE! I will not accept the "I will always have a car payment" mentality. I will not listen quietly to another person tell me, "I could never become financially free!"

IT DOES NOT HAVE TO BE THAT WAY!!!

Do you want to achieve your dreams? Even the big crazy ones? Do you want to achieve financial freedom and live a fully funded life? Read on! Apply the principles taught within these pages. Prepare a plan that will move you from where you are right now to where you want to be in the future. Write it down. Put it on the refrigerator. Make it highly visible. Get moving! If you want to achieve the thing you were put on this earth to do, you must have a plan. Make it happen! It will not just happen by itself. If God called you to do it, by all means GO DO IT!

Before you move on to the next chapter, use the "Dreams List" on the following page to list the reasons you want to achieve financial freedom. It will take a few minutes, but it will be worth it! When you are done, tear the page out and place it on your refrigerator as a public declaration and reminder of why you are going to become an expert at managing your money. Even more, completing this step will help you accomplish Rung #1 of the IWBNIN Ladder.

You can do this!

Dreams List
I want to achieve financial freedom so I can …

6 It's EZ™ To Budget!

Budget???!!! If this word alarms you, please do not close this book now. Do not burn this book. PLEASE read on. I promise you this material will change your life!

When I ask people if they have a written budget, they develop a problem with the corners of their lips as they tend to form a sneer and respond with a resounding, "NO!"

I have found for many people, the word "budget" is a very close cousin to the words "frustrating", "exhausting", and "impossible." This is usually a result of their past budgeting attempts.

They have tried budgeting, but it did not work out very well for them. Their spouse handed them a budget and announced that the family was now required to live by it. The monthly budget included a total of $3.45 for restaurants, $5.31 for groceries, and zero money was included for school clothes for the children. As a result, the budget was not realistic. Refusing to reflect reality within a monthly budget is the top reason a budget will fail to work for people.

Even if your past budgeting attempts have failed miserably, you will never regret the decision to institute a monthly budget that actually works. The reason I am so passionate about budgets is because my journey to a fully funded life would not have been possible without one.

In every family, it seems there is a spender and a saver. In my family, I am the spender and Jenn is a saver.

Because I am a spender, I chose to manage our finances because it allowed me to have direct control of the accounts. This conveniently ensured I would know if we had any extra money so I could spend it. This was a very bad plan!

About four months after making the commitment that we were going to work together on our finances, Jenn walked in to our living room holding a piece of paper with handwriting on it.

"What do you think of this budget?" she asked, interrupting the TV program I was watching.

True to my spending nature, a sneer automatically formed on my face as I said, "A budget?" I was thinking, "A budget? I don't need no stinking budget!"

"We need something to make our money behave," Jenn said.

Now, there are times in life where you will experience landmark moments. Moments you will look back on and note as life-changing. An event that changes your entire future. While we did not fully realize it at the time, Jenn had just created such a time for the Sangl family. She had latched us onto the financial tool that would allow us to win with money. I am forever grateful to Jenn for the way she handled this moment. She did not prepare the budget to get what she wanted. She did not write it up to control me. It was developed so *we* could win with our finances *together*.

Husbands who are reading this book please take note. Your bride is very wise and when she approaches you with an idea it should be treated as very valuable.

A prior attempt at budgeting …

I had tried budgeting before. It was an annual budget. I had prepared the budget to convince Jenn that we should purchase a brand new Honda Odyssey.

Income Item	Yearly	Monthly $	Category	
Joe	$ 70,700.00	$ 5,891.67	Income	
Jen	$ -	$ -	Income	
Total Income	$ 70,700.00	$ 5,891.67		
Expense Item	**Yearly**	**Monthly $**	**Category**	
Automobile - 1997 Truck	$ 3,000.00	$ 250.00	Auto	✓
Automobile - Mini-van	$ 6,600.00	$ 550.00	Auto	
Gasoline	$ 1,400.00	$ 116.67	Auto	✓
Insurance	$ 1,000.00	$ 83.33	Auto	
Maintenance	$ 1,000.00	$ 83.33	Auto	✓
Cable Television	$ 600.00	$ 50.00	Utility	
Electricity	$ 700.00	$ 58.33	Utility	✓
Garbage & Recycle	$ 180.00	$ 15.00	Utility	✓
Internet	$ 264.00	$ 22.00	Utility	
Natural Gas	$ 860.00	$ 71.67	Utility	✓
Telephone	$ 1,000.00	$ 83.33	Utility	✓
Water & Sewer	$ 500.00	$ 41.67	Utility	✓
Tithes	$ 7,100.00	$ 591.67	Charity	✓
Purdue University	$ 100.00	$ 8.33	Charity	✓
United Way	$ 780.00	$ 65.00	Charity	✓
Groceries	$ 5,200.00	$ 433.33	Food	
Dining Out	$ 1,000.00	$ 83.33	Food	✓
Gifts	$ 1,000.00	$ 83.33	Gifts	✓
Healthcare	$ 500.00	$ 41.67	Health	✓
Household	$ 1,000.00	$ 83.33	Household	✓
Health Insurance	$ 1,500.00	$ 125.00	Insurance	✓
Life Insurance	$ 530.00	$ 44.17	Insurance	✓
Mortgage	$ 10,800.00	$ 900.00	House	✓
YMCA	$ 700.00	$ 58.33	Health	
Miscellaneous Spending	$ 4,000.00	$ 333.33	Misc	
Vacation	$ 3,000.00	$ 250.00	Vacation	
Taxes	$ 20,000.00	$ 1,666.67	Taxes	
Clothing	$ 1,000.00	$ 83.33	Clothes	
401k	$ 5,656.00	$ 471.33	Investment	
Total Required	$ 80,970.00	$ 6,747.50		
Delta	$ (10,270.00)	$ (855.83)		

Handwritten notes: Could lower. (Insurance) • Could not get. (Cable Television) • Could not get. (Internet) • Could we lower? (Groceries) • Could we lower? / Could we lower. (YMCA / Miscellaneous Spending)

My Horrible Attempt At Annual Budgeting

Take a look at my annual budget. It does not even come close to balancing. Instead of addressing the huge car payment I was attempting to fit into the budget, I was cutting expenses that really did not amount to much. It was a classic case of ignoring the elephant in the room.

After listening to Jenn and her wise advice, we decided against purchasing the new car. My budget had failed (to get me the car), so I continued my bad feelings about budgets.

Now here Jenn was trying to convince me to try budgeting again. Although I did not feel like budgeting, I felt I should give it a try because my wife was cute. She had taken the time to write down some ideas for how to spend the next month's money. The least I could do was look at her work. Here's that exact budget she'd prepared.

Sangl Family's First-Ever Working Budget

One look at the budget got my attention. There was something highly unusual. It did not require debt! It did not require the use of credit cards. This was good since we had chopped those up several months earlier.

Even though I am a spender, I also am a trained engineer who loves math. I immediately saw how we could use Microsoft Excel to prepare the budget. Microsoft Excel spreadsheets have the capability to automatically update the math as you adjust income and expenses. It allows you to focus on financial decisions instead of conducting math exercises on a calculator.

As I prepared the budget in Microsoft Excel, I realized the MOST POWERFUL LESSON I have ever learned about managing my personal finances.

Before I share this lesson with you, it is important to note that I have a diploma from Southwestern High School, a Bachelor of Science in Mechanical Engineering from Purdue University, and a Masters of Business Administration from Clemson University. However, I had never learned this financial lesson before. I had received twenty years of formal education and never learned this lesson. TWENTY YEARS!!!

Are you ready for the lesson I learned? Please do not underestimate the POWER of this lesson. When I share it with you, it may seem really simplistic. It might even seem juvenile. It might be so ridiculously easy that you will think I am joking, but I am not. It is quite profound.

If you truly get this lesson and apply it, you will accomplish far more than you ever thought possible with your personal finances. If you do not apply it, your chances of succeeding will drop dramatically. No one is exempt from this lesson. It is a hard and fast rule!

Are you ready for the lesson that changed my life and can change yours too?

The lesson that forever changed Joe and Jenn Sangl's lives:

INCOME – OUTGO = EXACTLY ZERO™

$$I - O = EZ^{TM}$$

$$It's\ EZ^{TM}!$$

INCOME – OUTGO = EXACTLY ZERO™

No matter who you are, you cannot avoid this money fact. The last I checked, money still isn't growing on trees. It is finite. It is limited.

You might earn $1,000 a month. You may receive $5,000 a month. You could even make $20,000 a month. Regardless of the amount, it is limited.

If you make $20,000 a month and spend $20,000 of it, I can guarantee you will have $0 left. If you make $20,000 and spend $21,000, you will be forced to reduce your savings by $1,000 or utilize debt to spend the additional $1,000.

Now, you could use a printer to print $1,000 in money, but you will be introduced to a new home that comes complete with room and board – it is called prison! The $1,000 will not magically appear out of thin air to make up the difference. Only the federal government can legally print money.

Think for a moment about your monthly income. Whatever amount it may be, it is limited. That is a fact. Many people whine about needing to earn more before they can start saving. Don't be one of those people. Instead, focus on the fact that money is limited and make a commitment to maximize every single dollar. If you spend more than you make this month, you will be required to do one of two things to make up the difference: (1) consume your savings or (2) use debt.

INCOME – OUTGO = EXACTLY ZERO™

Look at the formula again. As a trained engineer, I was accustomed to derivatives, integrations, kernels, and other complex mathematical equations. This formula just seemed too easy for something as complex as money, but it really is this simple.

NOTE: The budgeting software demonstrated on the next few pages is available for FREE at www.IWBNIN.com – click on "Tools". The tools were created with Microsoft Excel, but any number of spreadsheet programs can be utilized. These budgeting tools will be used to teach you how to prepare a budget that actually works.

The most important key in preparing a budget that actually works is to plan your spending BEFORE you actually receive your income.

Step 1: *Prepare a list of all of your expected income and expenses for the upcoming month.*

Let's say a couple named Ron and Judy wants to start budgeting monthly. Their first step is to list all expected income and expenses.

INCOME	AMOUNT
Take Home Income	$4,000.00
OUTGO	
Charitable Gifts (Tithe)	$450.00
Emergency Fund	$300.00
Mortgage	$950.00
Electricity/Gas	$200.17
Water	$25.45
Cell Phone	$98.00
Trash	$25.00
Cable	$50.00
Groceries	$500.00
Dining Out	$200.00
Car Payment	$378.00
Gasoline	$200.00
License Plates	$16.67
Auto Insurance	$75.00
Oil Change	$35.00
Clothes – Children	$100.00
Doctor Bill	$125.14
Life Insurance	$40.00
Babysitting	$50.00
Spending Money	$150.00
Credit Card Bill	$175.00
Student Loan	$150.00
Entertainment (Basketball Game)	$74.00
TOTAL OUTGO	**$4,367.43**

As you can see, their expenses are greater than their income this month. Does this sound familiar? If so, don't start trimming expenses just yet. The goal of this first step is to document all of your household wants and needs for the upcoming month. You will make decisions on what will be included or excluded shortly.

I recommend you write these monthly wants/needs in a place where it is easily seen and accessed – particularly if you are married. It is much easier for both of you to contribute to the conversation if you can work on the same document. I have included a blank budget here for you to use. You can print out a larger copy by visiting www.IWBNIN.com – click on "Tools".

IT'S EZ™ TO BUDGET!

EZ™ Budget

TOTAL INCOME	
TOTAL OUTGO	
INCOME - OUTGO	

INCOME (Take Home Pay)	Amount
Income 1	
Income 2	
Income 3	
Income 4	

OUTGO (Actual Expenses)	Amount
Giving	
Charitable Organizations	
Gifts	
Christmas Gifts	

Saving	Amount
Emergency Fund	
Retirement Fund	
New Car Fund	
New Furniture Fund	
College Fund	
Wedding Fund	
Other:	
Other:	

Housing	Amount
Mortgage – 1st	
Mortgage – 2nd	
Rent	
Homeowner's Insurance	
Renter's Insurance	
Property Taxes	
Homeowner's Association Fees	
Electricity	
Natural Gas	
Telephone	
Cable TV – Satellite TV	
Internet	
Water	
Sewer	
Trash	
Other:	
Other:	

Transportation	Amount
Car Payment – 1	
Car Payment – 2	
Car Insurance	
Car License Plate Fees/Taxes	
Gasoline/Diesel	
Car Repairs	
Oil Change/Maintenance	

I WAS BROKE. NOW I'M NOT.

Food	Amount
Groceries	
Dining Out	
School Lunches	
Other:	

Clothing	Amount
Children	
Adults	
Other:	

Other Debts	Amount
Credit Card 1	
Credit Card 2	
Credit Card 3	
Credit Card 4	
Credit Card 5	
Student Loan 1	
Student Loan 2	
Student Loan 3	
Furniture	
Other:	
Other:	
Other:	
Other:	
Other:	
Other:	

Personal	Amount
Health Insurance	
Life Insurance	
Child Care	
Alimony	
Child Support	
Vacation	
Income Taxes	
Entertainment	
Cell Phone	
Medical Bill	
Spending Money	
Other:	
Other:	
Other:	

IT'S EZ™ TO BUDGET!

Step 2: *Enter your income and expenses into the free budget tool located at www.IWBNIN.com - click on "Tools"*

It is time to see where your money stands. You could certainly prepare a budget using paper, pencil and a calculator, but it is so much easier to enter the numbers into the budget tool and have it do the math for you.

TOTAL INCOME	4,000.00
TOTAL OUTGO	4,367.43
INCOME - OUTGO	-367.43

INCOME (Take Home Pay)	Amount
Income 1	4,000.00

OUTGO (Actual Expenses)	
Giving	**Amount**
Charitable Organizations	450.00

Saving	Amount
Emergency Fund	300.00

Housing	Amount
Mortgage – 1st	950.00
Electricity	200.17
Cable TV – Satellite TV	50.00
Water	25.45
Trash	25.00

Transportation	Amount
Car Payment – 1	378.00
Car Insurance	75.00
Car License Plate Fees/Taxes	16.67
Gasoline/Diesel	200.00
Oil Change/Maintenance	35.00

Food	Amount
Groceries	500.00
Dining Out	200.00

Clothing	Amount
Children	100.00

Other Debts	Amount
Credit Card 1	175.00
Student Loan 1	150.00

Personal	Amount
Life Insurance	40.00
Child Care	50.00
Entertainment	74.00
Cell Phone	98.00
Medical Bill	125.14
Spending Money	150.00

As the budget tool clearly reveals, the OUTGO exceeds INCOME by $367.43. This is not an EZ™ Budget. Are you starting to see the power of putting every expense on paper BEFORE the income (and the month) arrives? If you tried to budget after you have already received the income, your money would not necessarily be going where you really want it to go.

By putting every dollar on paper prior to receiving the income and before incurring the expenses, you will be given the power to make better choices regarding the use of the money. You will have control of your finances. Isn't this awesome? I told you that you could do this! It is not too hard. Go ahead and yell out loud, "I can do this!"

When I was in junior high school, students were required to participate in a class titled "I Can!" The course was written by the renowned motivational speaker, Zig Ziglar. While I don't remember too much about the class, I have never forgotten those two words: "I CAN!" Guess what? "YOU CAN!" I believe in you! I have seen so many people who previously thought "I can't" have their lives dramatically transformed through the application of this budget process. They now understand Henry Ford was quite right when he said, "Whether you think you can or you can't, you're right!"

Step 3: *Make INCOME – OUTGO = EXACTLY ZERO™*
Remember the formula? Here it is again. I really want you to get this. If you get nothing else from this book, I want you to apply this formula. After all, it's EZ™!

INCOME – OUTGO = EXACTLY ZERO™

In our example, Ron and Judy have entered their income and expected expenses into the budget tool and discovered they are facing a shortage of $367.43 for the upcoming month. Now, Ron and Judy *could* live this way for the month, but they would have to do one of the two things discussed earlier to cover the negative balance: (1) consume savings or (2) use debt.

Ron and Judy have committed to each other that they are going to win with their money. They are ready to make the changes necessary to achieve their long-term goals and live a fully funded life. Application of Income – Outgo = Exactly Zero™ means they must increase income or reduce outgo this month – or a combination of both.

Since Ron receives a fixed monthly salary, there is little opportunity for him to increase his income within the next month. Judy is focused on raising their children which makes it difficult for her to produce income right now. As a result, they decide that their income is fixed for this month. Ron is going to bring home $4,000. This is his take-home pay after paying taxes, health insurance premiums, retirement contributions, and other deductions. The $4,000 is what will be available to spend on household bills and expenses.

Since the income is not going to increase this month, adjustments must be made to their outgo. This means $367.43 must be eliminated from their planned expenses for next month.

INCOME – OUTGO = EXACTLY ZERO™

Let's review their expenses to understand what is absolutely necessary. Which ones do you think are absolutely necessary?

Opinions will vary, but at a minimum I believe the following items are necessary expenses for Ron and Judy:

- o **Housing** (plus utilities for the house – does not include luxuries like cable TV)
- o **Transportation** (gas, car payment, car insurance – does not include four car washes a month)
- o **Food** (ensure the family has enough to eat and be healthy – does not include restaurants)
- o **Clothing** (ensure the family has appropriate clothing – does not include the latest and greatest fashions or brands of clothing)

In Ron and Judy's case, they are able to pay these expenses. Their problem is like the vast majority of people. Their "wants list" exceeds their ability to pay for them. However, unlike the average person, Ron and Judy are now committed to making this an EZ™ Budget.

What expenses should they cut? I could ask 100 people this question, and I would receive 100 different answers. We are all different from each other. We value different things. The way in which we make decisions is different. This is fine as long as we end up with an EZ™ Budget.

So what did Ron and Judy do? Well, Ron and Judy decided they could cut back on their "Spending Money." They lowered it from $150 to $100. This reduced their budget deficit to $317.43.

TOTAL INCOME	4,000.00
TOTAL OUTGO	4,317.43
INCOME – OUTGO	-317.43

Ron and Judy then decided that instead of attending a basketball game and a movie this month, they would just attend the basketball game and watch some movies at home instead. They reduced their "Entertainment" fund from $74 to $40 making their budget only $283.43 short.

TOTAL INCOME	4,000.00
TOTAL OUTGO	4,283.43
INCOME – OUTGO	-283.43

Ron and Judy had $50 budgeted for childcare. They decided to exchange babysitting with Ken and Meg. This completely eliminates the babysitting cost. Bartering is a great way to save money. I love it! This reduced the deficit another $50. The budget is close to being EZ™!

TOTAL INCOME	4,000.00
TOTAL OUTGO	4,233.43
INCOME – OUTGO	-233.43

The children did not really need any new clothes during the upcoming month, but Judy thought it would be nice to buy a pair of shoes for one of them. They reduced the "Clothing" fund from $100 to $50. The gap is now $183.43!

TOTAL INCOME	4,000.00
TOTAL OUTGO	4,183.43
INCOME – OUTGO	-183.43

Dining out is fun, but Ron and Judy really are committed to getting out of debt and winning with their finances. They choose to reduce their "Dining Out" fund from $200 to $100. Their budget now stands at $83.43 short. Getting closer to EZ™!

TOTAL INCOME	4,000.00
TOTAL OUTGO	4,083.43
INCOME – OUTGO	-83.43

The grocery fund has previously absorbed a few movies that magically jumped into the cart while shopping at Wal-Mart. This month, Ron and Judy have decided they will not let this sort of impulsive spending destroy their grocery budget. They reduce the grocery budget from $500 to $450 bringing them only $33.43 away from EZ™!

TOTAL INCOME	4,000.00
TOTAL OUTGO	4,033.43
INCOME – OUTGO	-33.43

The oil change was for the car, but it has only been 3,000 miles since its last oil change. Ron and Judy decided to delay this maintenance for one month. The car could easily go one extra month without any real issue. The elimination of this $35 expense makes them now have an extra $1.57 in their budget!

TOTAL INCOME	4,000.00
TOTAL OUTGO	3,998.43
INCOME – OUTGO	+1.57

To give every dollar a name, Ron and Judy add the $1.57 back to the "Entertainment" fund taking it from $40.00 to $41.57.

TOTAL INCOME	4,000.00
TOTAL OUTGO	4,000.00
INCOME – OUTGO	0.00

OH MY GOODNESS!!! What just happened??!! Ron and Judy just made INCOME – OUTGO = EXACTLY ZERO™!!!!!!!! It is now an EZ™ Budget!!!

INCOME – OUTGO = EXACTLY ZERO™

TOTAL INCOME	4,000.00
TOTAL OUTGO	4,000.00
INCOME - OUTGO	0.00

INCOME (Take Home Pay)	Amount
Income 1	4,000.00

OUTGO (Actual Expenses)	
Giving	**Amount**
Charitable Organizations	450.00

Saving	Amount
Emergency Fund	300.00

Housing	Amount
Mortgage – 1st	950.00
Electricity	200.17
Cable TV – Satellite TV	50.00
Water	25.45
Trash	25.00

Transportation	Amount
Car Payment – 1	378.00
Car Insurance	75.00
Car License Plate Fees/Taxes	16.67
Gasoline/Diesel	200.00
Oil Change/Maintenance	0.00

Food	Amount
Groceries	450.00
Dining Out	100.00

Clothing	Amount
Children	50.00

Other Debts	Amount
Credit Card 1	175.00
Student Loan 1	150.00

Personal	Amount
Life Insurance	40.00
Child Care	0.00
Entertainment	41.57
Cell Phone	98.00
Medical Bill	125.14
Spending Money	100.00

Do you see how this process works? Did you see how Ron and Judy had to make some choices? Of course, they did not *have* to make their budget balance. They could have used $367.43 from savings and made the budget "balance." They could have used their credit cards to pay for $367.43 of their expenses and delayed making tough decisions, but they have had enough. They have realized the equation really is true!

INCOME – OUTGO = EXACTLY ZERO™

Ron and Judy have learned the single most powerful lesson I have ever learned about finances. You will not win until you make your money behave. The only effective way I have found to make this happen is through a written budget prepared every single month *before* the month begins.

Ron and Judy will still be able to live well!

How long do you believe it will take you to use this process to prepare your own EZ™ budget? It will probably take less time than you think. It usually takes between forty-five and sixty minutes to make a first EZ™ budget.

After someone has done this for three months in a row, it will take an average of twenty minutes to prepare an entire spending plan for the month. These few minutes will:

- Change your entire financial future!
- Allow you to retire someday!
- Allow mom to stay at home and raise the children
- Enable you to pay for your children's college education
- Position you to fund your dreams
- Allow you to live a fully funded life!

You probably spent more than twenty minutes thinking about where you were going to eat lunch today!

Step 4: *Live according to the EZ™ Budget.*

If Ron and Judy prepared this budget and then chose to spend money differently than planned, this budget would not work. Adding new expenses without eliminating others would crush their budget. They would again be forced to consume savings or turn to debt to make up the difference. It would also mean they wasted valuable time preparing a budget they did not even use.

Some people actually prepare a budget every month and routinely choose to ignore it. I have one question for these people: WHY BOTHER? I am serious. Why bother? Why would a person go through the trouble to read this book and prepare an EZ™ budget only to ignore it? For those people, I would say go ahead and live without this key part of your IWBNIN Ladder foundation for another five years. I have been there. I have prepared a budget that did not balance, and as an additional step of brilliance, I did not live by it. Guess what? It did not help me win with money.

You may not know anyone else who prepares a monthly budget. This should not matter to you because studies routinely reveal that most people are completely broke. They are certainly not doing as well as they would be if they chose to plan their finances. The act of planning your spending BEFORE you ever spend the money is so powerful! It enables you to take control of your finances. It gives you choices.

I will borrow Nike's marketing slogan as it pertains to preparing a monthly EZ™ Budget: **Just Do It!**®

How to Budget – Final Notes

Let's review the steps again.

Step 1. Prepare a list of all of your expected income and expenses for the upcoming month

Step 2. Enter your income and expenses into the free budget tool located at www.IWBNIN.com - click on "Tools"

Step 3. Make INCOME – OUTGO = EXACTLY ZERO™

Step 4. Live according to the EZ Budget™

You can do this! When I realized this was the ticket for Jenn and me to eliminate debt and become financially free, I was willing to walk over hot coals to do it. This process actually ended up helping our marriage.

If you haven't already, go ahead and create your own EZ™ budget. You will be on your way to living a fully funded life! And again, free copies of budgets are available at www.IWBNIN.com - click on "Tools".

You can do this!

7 Weekly Budgeting

Regardless of how often you are paid or how much you are paid, the simple fact remains true:

INCOME – OUTGO = EXACTLY ZERO™

Monthly budgeting is admittedly the easiest form of budgeting. This is why Rung #2 is focused on saving one month of expenses. Achievement of this rung allows you to convert to monthly budgeting – regardless of pay frequency.

However, I fully understand that most people just getting started up the IWBNIN Ladder are unable to sit down and pay all of their bills once a month and be done with it. I lived this way for years, and it was a tremendous challenge.

For most people, they must perform a delicate balancing act when paying their bills every month. Each paycheck is utilized to pay certain bills. For many couples paid twice a month, one of the pay periods is a period of "famine" and the other pay period is a period of "feast." A budget will resolve this issue.

This chapter will show you how to successfully budget when living paycheck to paycheck and receiving pay weekly, bi-monthly, every two weeks, or any other pay schedule delivering income to your household.

Let's go back to Ron and Judy's balanced budget from the previous chapter. Let's assume they are paid

$1,000 per week take-home pay. Additionally, they do not have enough money in their bank account to just sit down and write out all of the checks at once. This means they must balance their spending to align with the arrival of each paycheck.

Below are Ron and Judy's expenses for the month.

INCOME	AMOUNT	When?	
Take Home Income	4,000.00	$1,000/week	
OUTGO			
Charitable Gifts	450.00	All Month	
Emergency Fund	300.00	All Month	
Mortgage	950.00	15th	
Electricity/Gas	200.17	10th	
Water	25.45	15th	
Cell Phone	98.00	25th	
Trash	25.00	15th	
Cable	50.00	15th	
Groceries	450.00	All Month	
Dining Out	100.00	All Month	
Car Payment	378.00	10th	
Gasoline	200.00	All Month	
License Plates	16.67	Saving	$200/yr ($16.67/mo)
Auto Insurance	75.00	15th	
Clothes – Children	50.00	When Possible	
Doctor Bill	125.14	10th	
Life Insurance	40.00	10th	$480/yr ($40/mo)
Spending Money	100.00	All Month	
Credit Card Bill	175.00	20th	
Student Loan	150.00	10th	
Entertainment (Basketball Game)	41.57	When Possible	
TOTAL OUTGO	**4,000.00**		

Using the free Monthly Budget By Week located at www.IWBNIN.com (click on "Tools"), Ron and Judy need to assign their planned expenses to pay periods in a way that allows each bill to be paid on time or early.

Monthly EZ™ Budget – Weekly

	11/1	11/8	11/15	11/22	TOTAL
TOTAL INCOME	1,000.00	1,000.00	1,000.00	1,000.00	4,000.00
TOTAL OUTGO	566.71	1,218.62	1,650.00	564.67	4,000.00
INCOME - OUTGO	+433.29	-218.62	-650.00	+435.33	0.00

INCOME (Take Home Pay)	Amount	Amount	Amount	Amount	Amount
Income 1	1,000.00	1,000.00	1,000.00	1,000.00	4,000.00

OUTGO (Actual Expenses)					
Giving	Amount	Amount	Amount	Amount	Amount
Charitable Organizations	112.50	112.50	112.50	112.50	450.00

Saving	Amount	Amount	Amount	Amount	Amount
Emergency Fund	75.00	75.00	75.00	75.00	300.00

Housing	Amount	Amount	Amount	Amount	Amount
Mortgage – 1st			950.00		950.00
Electricity		200.17			200.17
Cable TV – Satellite TV			50.00		50.00
Water		25.45			25.45
Trash		25.00			25.00

Transportation	Amount	Amount	Amount	Amount	Amount
Car Payment – 1		378.00			378.00
Car Insurance			75.00		75.00
Car License Plate Fees/Taxes				16.67	16.67
Gasoline/Diesel	50.00	50.00	50.00	50.00	200.00

Food	Amount	Amount	Amount	Amount	Amount
Groceries	112.50	112.50	112.50	112.50	450.00
Dining Out	25.00	25.00	25.00	25.00	100.00

Clothing	Amount	Amount	Amount	Amount	Amount
Children				50.00	50.00

Other Debts	Amount	Amount	Amount	Amount	Amount
Credit Card 1			175.00		175.00
Student Loan 1		150.00			150.00

Personal	Amount	Amount	Amount	Amount	Amount
Life Insurance		40.00			40.00
Entertainment	41.57				41.57
Cell Phone				98.00	98.00
Medical Bill	125.14				125.14
Spending Money	25.00	25.00	25.00	25.00	100.00

Ron and Judy's budget is an EZ™ budget *overall*. However, each week does not equal Exactly Zero™. Knowing money does not grow on trees, this is a problem!

While confident the overall monthly budget has enough money to pay all of their bills, they must now work to develop an EZ™ budget for each paycheck.

Their 11/8 and 11/15 paychecks are overspent while the 11/1 and 11/22 paychecks are underspent. They begin to look for areas where expenses could be moved from their overspent paychecks to those that are underspent.

Ron and Judy decide to move their Emergency Buffer Fund savings from the first three paychecks to their final check of the month – the 11/22 paycheck.

	11/1	11/8	11/15	11/22	TOTAL
TOTAL INCOME	1,000.00	1,000.00	1,000.00	1,000.00	4,000.00
TOTAL OUTGO	491.71	1,143.62	1,575.00	789.67	4,000.00
INCOME – OUTGO	+508.29	-143.62	-575.00	+210.33	0.00
Emergency Buffer Fund	0.00	0.00	0.00	300.00	300.00

Ron and Judy then choose to move $508.29 of their $950 House Mortgage Payment to 11/1. This makes the 11/1 budget EZ™, but the other three pay periods are not balanced.

	11/1	11/8	11/15	11/22	TOTAL
TOTAL INCOME	1,000.00	1,000.00	1,000.00	1,000.00	4,000.00
TOTAL OUTGO	1,000.00	1,143.62	1,066.71	789.67	4,000.00
INCOME – OUTGO	0.00	-143.62	-66.71	+210.33	0.00
Mortgage – 1st	508.29		441.71		950.00

Ron and Judy move all of their Spending Money from their first three paychecks to the 11/22 paycheck.

	11/1	11/8	11/15	11/22	TOTAL
TOTAL INCOME	1,000.00	1,000.00	1,000.00	1,000.00	4,000.00
TOTAL OUTGO	975.00	1,118.62	1,041.71	864.67	4,000.00
INCOME – OUTGO	+25.00	-118.62	-41.71	+135.33	0.00
Spending Money	0.00	0.00	0.00	100.00	50.00

Because Ron and Judy have a pantry and freezer full of food that has accumulated over time, they decide to skip one week of grocery shopping. This decision has the added benefit of a cleaner pantry and freezer! They move the $112.50 grocery expenditure from the 11/8 paycheck to the 11/22 budget.

	11/1	11/8	11/15	11/22	TOTAL
TOTAL INCOME	1,000.00	1,000.00	1,000.00	1,000.00	4,000.00
TOTAL OUTGO	1,000.00	1,006.12	1,041.71	977.17	4,000.00
INCOME – OUTGO	+25.00	-6.12	-41.71	+22.83	0.00
Groceries	112.50	0.00	112.50	225.00	450.00

Because Dining Out is a discretionary expense, Ron and Judy decide to redistribute their Dining Out money to help move their individual paycheck budgets closer to EZ™. See their adjustments below.

	11/1	11/8	11/15	11/22	TOTAL
TOTAL INCOME	1,000.00	1,000.00	1,000.00	1,000.00	4,000.00
TOTAL OUTGO	983.29	1,000.00	1,016.71	1,000.00	4,000.00
INCOME – OUTGO	+16.71	0.00	-16.71	0.00	0.00
Dining Out	33.29	18.88	0.00	47.83	100.00

Two paychecks are now balanced to Exactly Zero™! Only two more to go. As they reviewed their budget, Ron and Judy felt that since they were going to skip one week of grocery shopping, they would prefer to have a little extra food money the first week. This would help them have enough money to purchase perishable items during their "interesting meals from the freezer and pantry" week. They decide to move $16.71 in grocery money from the 11/15 budget to 11/1.

	11/1	11/8	11/15	11/22	TOTAL
TOTAL INCOME	1,000.00	1,000.00	1,000.00	1,000.00	4,000.00
TOTAL OUTGO	1,000.00	1,000.00	1,000.00	1,000.00	4,000.00
INCOME – OUTGO	0.00	0.00	0.00	0.00	0.00
Groceries	129.21	0.00	95.79	225.00	450.00

I WAS BROKE. NOW I'M NOT.

Success! They now have an EZ Budget™ for every paycheck! By working together to budget before the month began, Ron and Judy have been able to achieve INCOME – OUTGO = EXACTLY ZERO™ for every single paycheck! All of their payments will be made on time and every single financial obligation has been met!

Monthly EZ Budget™ – Weekly

	11/1	11/8	11/15	11/22	TOTAL
TOTAL INCOME	1,000.00	1,000.00	1,000.00	1,000.00	4,000.00
TOTAL OUTGO	1,000.00	1,000.00	1,000.00	1,000.00	4,000.00
INCOME - OUTGO	0.00	0.00	0.00	0.00	0.00
INCOME (Take Home Pay)	Amount	Amount	Amount	Amount	Amount
Income 1	1,000.00	1,000.00	1,000.00	1,000.00	4,000.00
OUTGO (Actual Expenses)					
Giving	Amount	Amount	Amount	Amount	Amount
Charitable Organizations	112.50	112.50	112.50	112.50	450.00
Saving	Amount	Amount	Amount	Amount	Amount
Emergency Fund				300.00	300.00
Housing	Amount	Amount	Amount	Amount	Amount
Mortgage – 1st	508.29		441.71		950.00
Electricity		200.17			200.17
Cable TV – Satellite TV			50.00		50.00
Water		25.45			25.45
Trash		25.00			25.00
Transportation	Amount	Amount	Amount	Amount	Amount
Car Payment – 1		378.00			378.00
Car Insurance			75.00		75.00
Car License Plate Fees/Taxes				16.67	16.67
Gasoline/Diesel	50.00	50.00	50.00	50.00	200.00
Oil Change/Maintenance					0.00
Food	Amount	Amount	Amount	Amount	Amount
Groceries	129.21		95.79	225.00	450.00
Dining Out	33.29	18.88		47.83	100.00
Clothing	Amount	Amount	Amount	Amount	Amount
Children				50.00	50.00
Other Debts	Amount	Amount	Amount	Amount	Amount
Credit Card 1			175.00		175.00
Student Loan 1		150.00			150.00
Personal	Amount	Amount	Amount	Amount	Amount
Life Insurance		40.00			40.00
Child Care	0.00				0.00
Entertainment	41.57				41.57
Cell Phone				98.00	98.00
Medical Bill	125.14				125.14
Spending Money				100.00	100.00

Now you may be saying, "Joe, how could they just skip a week without buying groceries? That is not possible!"

My answer is that Ron and Judy are no longer normal. They can easily go one week without purchasing groceries by using the food in their freezer and pantry. Besides, they have a week to prepare for the one without grocery money. Because they planned *before* the month began, they are able to see the financial challenges they will face during the second week of the month. This gave them the opportunity to adjust their grocery spending. By living frugally, they will have money left over in the grocery fund from the first week to utilize during the second week.

Did you catch the part about Ron and Judy *having a plan* BEFORE spending their money?!!! They have a PLAN before they ever receive the actual cash. I cannot emphasize this point enough. By having a plan, Ron and Judy can work together to ensure they prepare appropriately for upcoming budget crunches.

This is the beauty of the budgeting process! You are able to manage your money instead of feeling like your money is managing you. You are telling your money where to go instead of wondering where it went!

What if Ron and Judy were paid only two times during the month? They would enter their take-home income into the budget tool and prepare a budget for each of their two paychecks and make the equation INCOME – OUTGO = EXACTLY ZERO™ true for each one.

How to Budget Weekly or Bi-Weekly – Final Notes

Let's review the steps again.

Step 1.	Prepare a list of all of your expected income and expenses for the upcoming month
Step 2.	Enter your income and expenses into the free monthly by week budget tool located at www.IWBNIN.com - click on "Tools"
Step 3.	Make INCOME – OUTGO = EXACTLY ZERO™
Step 4.	Make each individual paycheck an EZ Budget™.
Step 5.	Live according to the EZ Budget™

It is that simple! I *love* this stuff! It's so EZ™!

You can do this!

8 Seasonal Budgeting

Budgeting when income is irregular/cyclical/seasonal

Many self-employed people and business owners know all too well the challenges of prospering with irregular income. In the lawn-care business, grass just stops growing during winter. In the summer, it will not stop growing and work seems endless. If you work in the retail industry, you may experience a Christmas shopping rush followed by a post-Christmas drought. The beach tourism industry experiences massive business during the summer vacation season and feel deserted as the fall approaches.

Unpredictable income is a reality for many people. When I provide financial coaching for people with this type of income, most of them believe it is impossible to budget. They say, "We can't budget, Joe. We don't even know what our income will be from month to month." I respond with, "It is possible. In fact, you need a budget more than anyone!"

If you have irregular, seasonal, and cyclical income, the following steps will help you prepare a budget and begin thriving financially. In fact, these are the very steps I use for my businesses. All of them experience crazy swings in income. This process has allowed us to prosper even during challenging business periods. If you feel like your irregular income is about to drive you crazy, take these steps. It will change your life.

Step 1: *Recognize it!*

You must recognize that you have irregular income. If you have ever starved to death during the off-season, you know what I am talking about. In order to stop having your life severely impacted by these down periods, you must acknowledge that your income goes up and down.

Step 2: *Determine your monthly salary requirement.*

In this step, you are really determining the monthly salary your business needs to pay you each month. The ultimate goal is to be able to pay yourself a fixed amount every single month.

This eliminates the crazy process of saying, "How much is in the business bank account? Okay, let's pay ourselves half of it." This constant pay variation will drive the bill payer in the family absolutely nuts. It also makes it very difficult to win with money.

To assist you in determining your monthly salary, download the free "Monthly Budget" tool at www.IWBNIN.com (click on "Tools"), and enter the following items:

A. **Fixed Expenses** Enter all of your fixed expenses including house payment, utilities, gasoline, car payments, credit card payments, groceries, cell phone, childcare, etc. These fixed expenses should also include long-term items such as retirement contributions and college savings.
B. **Variable Expenses** Enter the monthly average of your variable expenses such as clothing, spending money, entertainment, dining out, etc.
C. **Known, Upcoming Non-monthly Expenses** This is a key step! If you do not add in all of your known, upcoming non-monthly expenses (like annual taxes,

quarterly insurance premiums, vacation, car repairs and maintenance, birthdays, anniversaries, and Christmas), you will continue to live the feast/famine lifestyle. I call these types of expenses "budget-busters" because they will destroy your budget if you fail to save for them.

To accommodate these types of budget crushing expenses, I save for them monthly. Using the "Known Upcoming Expenses" calculator at www.IWBNIN.com, I identify all of my known, upcoming non-monthly expenses and place their annual cost next to them. The calculator divides this overall amount by twelve to determine how much I need to save every month.

Example of Known, Upcoming Non-monthly Expenses

	Annual Expense	Monthly Expense
Christmas	1,000	83
Health Club	780	65
Life Insurance	780	65
Auto Insurance	1,080	90
Vacation	2,160	180
Total	5,800	483

By saving $483 each month, it greatly reduces the chances that non-monthly expenses will cause a budget to fail. It also ensures that fun things like vacation and Christmas will be fully funded.

Accommodating these known, upcoming non-monthly expenses is covered in much greater detail in the Saving chapter.

D. **Income** Now that you have identified your monthly financial need (salary), all you need to do is add the income to the top of the budget to make it EZ™. You now have a monthly budget that will change very little throughout the year!

Now, of course, the trick is to have enough cash on hand every month to make this monthly budget work. The next step will position you to do this.

Step 3: *Save at least three months salary in Known Slumps Fund.*

WHAT?!!!! Perhaps this is what you are saying right now. I know it may be hard to consider having this amount of money sitting in your savings account, but it is indeed possible. It won't be especially easy, but you will have completely changed your life when you accomplish this step. You will be on your way to a *fully funded life*!

Once you have determined your monthly salary requirement in Step 2, simply multiply that number by three to determine your Known Slumps Fund Requirement. This is the targeted amount for you to have in savings at the beginning of your known slumps period – that period when you know income becomes quite a challenge to produce. For a lawn care specialist, this is the beginning of winter.

This money is called the "Known Slumps Fund" because you know slumps are coming. Since you know the slumps are coming, be financially prepared for them. This goes a long way toward eliminating the horrible feast/famine lifestyle so many people feel trapped in.

You might be asking, "Why on earth should I save up at least three months worth of expenses in a Known Slumps Fund?" I am so glad you asked!

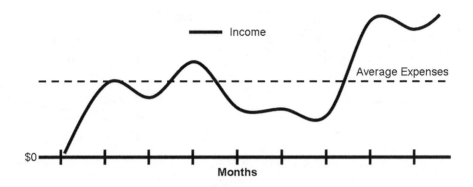

Let's say in Step 2, you calculated a monthly salary requirement of $3,000. This means you would need at least $9,000 in your Known Slumps Fund.

Suppose the following table outlines a year of income for your business.

Month	Business/Job Income
January	0
February	3,250
March	2,750
April	4,000
May	1,000
June	1,000
July	250
August	7,500
September	7,000
October	7,500
November	1,000
December	1,250
TOTAL	36,500

A monthly salary requirement of $3,000 per month is $36,000 per year. A quick look at the above income of $36,500 reveals that there will be enough money to pay the monthly salary, but look at how irregular the income is!

Have you seen something like this before in your business? This can cause life to be very stressful. Because January did not produce any income, you are required to eat ramen noodles like they are going out of style.

73

February through April are better, but you're having to catch up on the mess created by January. Then income dies again May through July. This is a famine of the worst degree! The business turns around as great income is produced August through October. Feasts abound and your household bills are caught back up. Then November and December come in back to back with terrible results. Back to the ramen noodles!

A Known Slumps Fund equal to three times your monthly salary requirement completely fixes the craziness this creates for your household. Let's see what difference it would have made if you would have had $9,000 stored up in your Known Slumps Fund as the year started out.

Month	Starting Known Slumps Fund Balance:			9,000
	Business/Job Income	Household Salary	Gain (LOSS)	Known Slumps Fund Balance
January	0	3,000	(3,000)	6,000
February	3,250	3,000	250	6,250
March	2,750	3,000	(250)	6,000
April	4,000	3,000	1,000	7,000
May	1,000	3,000	(2,000)	5,000
June	1,000	3,000	(2,000)	3,000
July	250	3,000	(2,750)	250
August	7,500	3,000	2,500	4,750
September	7,000	3,000	4,000	8,750
October	7,500	3,000	4,500	13,250
November	1,000	3,000	(2,000)	11,250
December	1,250	3,000	(1,750)	9,500
TOTAL	36,500	36,000		

When you look at this chart you realize the POWER of having three months of expenses in the bank! Whether you experienced a $250 income month or a $7,500 income month, you chose to live on your $3,000 salary each month. It ensures that you get to eat and pay all your bills every month. It allows you to save money (remember the monthly expenses included retirement and college savings). You can even have some fun each month!

The Known Slumps Fund absorbs the irregularities of your income and prevents it from destroying your household finances. Take the actions required to fill up your Known Slumps Fund. It eliminates so much stress from your life!

If I had not taken the step of incorporating a Known Slumps Fund for my businesses to secure my monthly salary requirement, I am confident our businesses and household finances would have failed. It would have driven my bride and me completely crazy, and we would have had to endure tons of unnecessary stress and anguish.

If you own a business, it is important to maintain a Known Slumps Fund at least for the business because the business secures your income. Ideally, you would have this fund established for both the business and your household.

If you are not a business owner, but the nature of your employment creates highly irregular income – like a high commission sales job, hair stylist, restaurant server, or a real estate agent, you actually need to function as a business and establish a separate bank account for your income. This serves two functions. First: It allows you to eliminate the intermingling of business income and expenses with your household income and expenses. This eliminates a certain level of headaches created by trying to determine which transactions are business-related and which ones are household. Second: Combining this money together with your household spending account will put your Known Slumps Fund at risk of being used for something else. Separate bank accounts allow you to pay a monthly salary to your household account while protecting money remaining in the Known Slumps Fund.

How do you build up your Known Slumps Fund? Sell some possessions. Eliminate some monthly bills for a while. Work an extra job on the side. Have a blow out sale on some merchandise sitting in inventory. Whatever you do, do it quickly. The sooner you establish this fund, the more swiftly you will be able to move away from the chaos of living with crazy and unpredictable income.

Step 4: *Become personally debt-free.*

What happens to your monthly expenses when you have no debt payments? They go down. Way down. For a large majority of Americans, non-house debt payments are at least 10% of their monthly expenses. If you include the house payment, these debt payments are 35% or more of a household's monthly expenses. Imagine what your life looks like without any debt!

This step allows you to apply more of your monthly salary toward investments which will help you live a more fully funded life. While a less popular option, it can also reduce your monthly salary requirement thereby decreasing the amount needed for your Known Slumps Fund. Isn't this EZ™?

How to Budget with Seasonal Income – Summary

Step 1.   Recognize it!

Step 2.   Determine your monthly salary requirement.

Step 3.   Save at least three months salary in Known Slumps Fund.

Step 4.   Become personally debt-free.

If you apply these steps, you will be able to pay yourself a fixed monthly salary that allows your family and business to prosper for the long term.

You can do this!

9 Budgeting Tips

Budgeting Tips

There are some key strategies that can be very useful in the process of developing a hugely successful INCOME – OUTGO = EXACTLY ZERO™ budget. Apply these tips within your own budget, and it will accelerate your climb up the IWBNIN Ladder. This, of course, will help you live a fully funded life.

Give

Did you notice Ron and Judy's budget had $450 included in the charitable contributions category? This is because something incredible happens when you gain control of your finances. You begin to have control over where your money goes. No longer must all of the money go toward credit card payments, car payments, furniture payments, student loans, and other debts.

As you become debt-free, you *free* up money. This provides you with choices. I love choices. Everyone loves choices!

Ron and Judy love their church. They have decided to employ the biblical principle of tithing – which is the spiritual and financial practice of giving the first ten percent of household gross income to God. Because this is something they believe in deeply, they are excited to finally be able to support it. An EZ™ budget was key to ensuring their giving happens each and every month.

What cause do you passionately believe in? Would the organization or individual benefit from your financial support? Have you been able to support it like you want to? A written budget will allow you to make this choice more easily.

Giving is the favorite part of my budget. In fact, as Jenn and I became debt-free, we began including an additional line item called "bless others" each month. This is money we allocate for spontaneously helping others. It has been amazing to see how this money has opened our eyes to very real needs in our community. To be able to help out financially is such a rewarding experience.

Save

Did you also notice Ron and Judy are saving $200 for their emergency fund? They have discovered that unexpected expenses sometimes crop up *during* the month. Surprise expenses like a flat tire on their car. This saved money is not for impulse purchases such as a beautiful couch on sale for thirty percent off. Nor is it for going to the movies or a baseball game that was not included in the budget.

When an unexpected expense crops up that is truly an emergency, they will be able to pay for it without blowing up the monthly budget or having to utilize debt. It's an amazing thing to actually have a plan for emergencies.

By the way, you are the only person who can make savings happen for your household. The government will not help you save. Children definitely will not help! Make it your habit to include savings in your budget every single month.

It is important to give every dollar a name.

Did you notice every dollar and cent has a name? Did it seem ridiculous to do this? Did it seem abnormal? It should! As Dave Ramsey, the great financial teacher says, "Normal is B-R-O-K-E. Choose to be weird."

Now, I am not saying you should list every single item you are planning to purchase. A toothbrush costing $2.43 does not deserve it's own line in the budget. Instead, place the expenses into reasonable groups. For example, my family considers all grocery, toiletries, and household items as one category – groceries. We do this because we generally purchase all of these items at the same store. If a spending category is less than $10 for the month, it should probably be included together with some other group.

Give every dollar a name and spend it as planned. It will give you better control of your money and help you begin living a fully funded life.

If married, work together on your financial plans.

Did you notice Ron and Judy worked on their budget TOGETHER? My marriage became unbelievably better when we started budgeting together. Why? Because we had to discuss our spending. We had to communicate. This required some "for better or worse" discussions, but guess what? We had to go through some "for worse" discussions so now we can have the "for better" discussions. We had to agree on how we were going to give, save, invest, and spend our money.

We have had to discuss when the nephews and nieces have their birthdays, graduations, and weddings because we want to send a gift to each one of them. It costs money. A side benefit of these conversations: I actually know when these nephews and nieces are having a special day! I used to be the person who was thanked by their nephews/nieces for a present they had received and responded, "You're welcome!" Then I would immediately turn to Jenn and ask, "What did we send them and why?" Now, I really know!

We have had to make hard decisions – HARD DECISIONS – like what we were going to cut out of the budget in order to pay cash for very costly and unplanned surgeries. We could have utilized our emergency fund for those surgeries, but we knew we would have four months until the insurance companies would finally process the medical bills. If we worked together and buckled down our budgeting process for those four months, we could pay cash for the medical bills without impacting our emergency fund. We even discovered that paying cash within 30 days of receiving the final doctor bill allowed us to receive a ten percent discount! We did not even have to ask for it. It was part of the fine print written on the bill.

Jenn and I also make joint spending decisions on vacations, gifts, retirement contributions, college savings, and charitable giving. These are amazing discussions that enable us to better understand each other and help us work on our future plans TOGETHER!

Cash Envelopes

Cash envelopes are one of the key reasons Jenn and I are able to stick to our budget each month. Studies repeatedly show you will spend less if you pay with cash. When you pay with cash, it helps you truly understand that money is limited and finite.

Pull out your credit card and place a $100 bill next to it. Which one is your eye drawn to? Which would you rather have? Guess what? It's the same one that retailers want from you! Cash!

Compare McDonald's cash transactions versus their debit/credit card transactions. The average debit and credit card transaction amount is over 40% more than the average dollar amount of each cash transaction.

Burger King shared the following fact in an annual report. "Visa and MasterCard studies show that the average ticket size of ... purchases made with credit cards exceeds that of cash transactions – about 30% more according to Visa."[1]

The use of a cash envelope system is most effective for impulsive spending categories. I use cash envelopes for groceries, dining out, clothing, spending money, and entertainment.

By utilizing cash, I am able to separate impulsive spending categories from my bank account. It also means I don't have to keep track of how much I have spent for each category. I can simply count the cash I have left. As a natural spender, all I want to know is how much is remaining for me to spend anyway!

Consider this thought. Do I care if the grocery fund started out with $450? Absolutely not. All I care about is that the envelope has $73 remaining for the rest of the month. If I have five days left before the month ends, then we are in great shape. If we have 20 days left, we are in big trouble! In either case, I know I will never exceed the budgeted amount because I am using cash. We will not use the debit card or withdraw cash and violate our EZ™ Budget!

How to implement the Cash Envelope System:

1. **Identify your cash envelopes** Determine the spending categories in which you tend to be

---

[1] www.digitaltransactions.net/files/acq.doc *Fast Food Cooks up a Winning Card Recipe* by Lauri Giesen

"impulsive," and establish a cash envelope for each one. You can utilize regular mailing envelopes with the category written on the outside or purchase any number of great cash envelope wallets available on-line.

2. **On payday, withdraw cash for your envelopes** Using your budget, determine the amount of cash to withdraw for each envelope. Obtain varying denominations of money so you can divide it appropriately among the envelopes.

3. **Utilize cash envelope money for the assigned spending category** Use "grocery" envelope money for your food purchases. When you go to a restaurant, use your "dining out" cash.

4. **Stop spending when the cash runs out** When the cash is gone, you have reached the budgeted spending limit. This is not the moment to pull out the debit or credit card. It is a time to stop spending!

Repeat this process each month. You will be amazed at how much money you will save. I saved $200 per month on "grocery spending" alone. Prior to cash envelopes, I would walk into Wal-Mart to purchase a gallon of milk and walk out with $80 worth of stuff and a fishing pole! Cash envelopes help ensure I do not blow up my budget.

What if I don't know the EXACT amount of some bills?
There are many items you may need to estimate for your budget. A few of them may include usage-based utilities like electricity, natural gas, water, sewer, etc. Others may need to be estimated because it is difficult or impossible to know the number exactly. This would also include items like groceries and gasoline.

What should you do? Estimate the cost. You can probably get within $10 of the actual cost for the month. If it is an item you will use an online bill payment service or a written check to pay, then this could become a problem if you do not keep track of your checking account or maintain a low balance.

One thing that helps this to NEVER become a problem for Jenn and me is we maintain a cushion in the checking account of at least $200 to $300. Because of this, I do not have to track my account balance every single day. This extra money does not give us a license to spend it. If a bill costs more than we have budgeted, we change the rest of our spending to ensure our plan remains EZ™!

In Ron and Judy's budget, they have budgeted an estimate for their groceries of $450. If they would have budgeted $500, they would have spent exactly $500. However, because they budgeted $450 and are using cash envelopes, they will now spend exactly $450. There is power in a having a plan!

How to handle an unexpected emergency

You will experience financial emergencies. It is a fact of life, and I have discovered these emergencies tend to arise when we can least afford them!

If you are married, discuss it with your spouse. If you are single, seek wise counsel from someone who is winning with money. Verify it truly is an emergency. Right now, what would be a financial emergency for you: A transmission failure on your car? What about replacing tires? How about seeing a great price on that new couch I mentioned earlier? What if it is paying for Christmas gifts without having saved for then? What about a sudden health issue?

Replacing car tires should not be an emergency. Car tire replacement is a known upcoming non-monthly expense. Tires wear out. We drive the car. The rubber wears off. Eventually, they must be replaced. This should not be an emergency. However, if you have not already saved for tires, replacing them could be a financial emergency.

Christmas should also not be an emergency. It is always on December 25th. Every year you have an entire twelve months to prepare for it. Again, if you have not chosen to save for this known upcoming expense, it could indeed become a financial emergency.

In reality, I can not tell you what exactly qualifies as a financial emergency for your family. Only you can do this. You should take a few minutes to determine what is truly a financial emergency for your household. These challenging moments are what will make your emergency fund money eligible for use. I encourage you to write down the events you believe qualify for use of these funds. Do this now while life is not in a state of emergency. This way, when the actual emergency arises, you will not feel guilty about utilizing the emergency fund for it.

Use the worksheet on the next page to document events that will qualify for use of your emergency fund.

I/We, the undersigned, hereby agree that the below events are classified as "EMERGENCIES". Emergency Fund money can be used to pay for these events.

Signature 1   **Signature 2**

How do I budget for non-monthly expenses?

Whenever anyone starts to force their money to behave, they experience "budget-busting" expenses. Many times these are non-monthly expenses. Expenses like auto and life insurance, property taxes, homeowner's insurance, vacations, Christmas, and special days can blow up the budget.

Should any of these expenses be a surprise? NO! If we stop and think about it, these are *known* expenses. Yet, somehow we allow them to become budget-crushing expenses. I have lived without budgeting for these types of expenses. It makes money management very challenging!

I have found the best way to manage these types of expenses is to save for them each time you are paid. A detailed process for implementing this is outlined in the Saving chapter.

When budget-busting expenses show up, do not give up! You are starting to make your money behave. You need to prepare for several of these budget-busting expenses to impact your first few budgets heavily.

What if I get paid weekly or bi-weekly and can't do just a monthly budget?

You should prepare an EZ™ budget for each paycheck within the month. See the chapter on weekly budgeting.

Of course, once you have accomplished Rung #2 of the IWBNIN Ladder, you can switch to the far easier monthly budget method.

What if I have a highly seasonal income, can I budget?

Many have used this as an excuse to avoid creating a budget. It's a lousy excuse! People using this excuse will continue to lose financially until they force their money to behave. See the chapter on seasonal budgeting.

Give yourself a raise. Save money in your budget.

How much money do you need to earn to bring home $100 extra dollars? The answer is approximately $150 because Uncle Sam takes his share. For the average family, one-third of pay goes toward taxes, and the other two-thirds is brought home. Two-thirds of $150 is $100.

How much money do you need to save in your budget to free up $100 to spend on something else or to save? The answer is exactly $100 because the money has already been taxed! In other words, if you manage to reduce your grocery spending by $100 per month, this savings is equivalent to receiving a pay raise of $150 per month!

Suppose by budgeting, you manage to spend $300 less per month. This is the same as receiving a $450 per month pay raise. If this savings is maintained for an entire year, it becomes the equivalent of an annual pay raise of $5,400!

This becomes easier as you go along.

The first month may be tough. The second month will be a little easier. The third month is even smoother. After a complete year of monthly budgeting, you will have absorbed the entire blast of "budget-busting" costs.

After one year of forcing your money to behave, you will have experienced amazing and hope-inspiring changes in your life and in your finances! HOPE will be restored. You will have a plan. You will be managing your money instead of the money managing you!

I just cannot write in words the LIFE-CHANGING impact this can have on your life. Jenn and I will never be the same. Never **EVER** be the same.

Having an emergency fund is important.

My great-aunt, Aunt La, always said it was nice to have a little jingle in your pocket. In other words, it is nice to have financial margin in your life. If you do not have a cash emergency fund, you will always be at risk of turning to debt when financial emergencies arise.

If Ron and Judy have no savings, anything could become a financial emergency. They could have a flat tire and need to replace it. Where will the money come from? If they have nothing saved, they will be highly tempted to utilize debt.

With $4,000 in their emergency fund (Rung #2), they could decide the flat tire qualifies as an emergency and avoid debt. The emergency fund provides breathing room, and it will remove stress. Think about the following question for at least ten seconds:

Question: How will it feel when you accomplish Rung #2 by having a month's worth of income in your savings account?

Wow! As I think about the first time I achieved this, I still get the same feeling of relief I had back then. It is an unbelievable feeling! It is a freeing feeling! Do you agree?

Now think about another question for 10 seconds:

Question: How would it feel to accomplish Rung #5 by having three months of expenses in your savings account?

Unbelievable, right? It is so liberating! When you achieve Rung #5, you are freed up. You are no longer consumed with the "how on earth am I going to get ahead?" question. You are able to focus on what you were put on this earth to do!

Guess what? You can do this! You really can accomplish Rung #5, and it can happen sooner than you think possible.

Avoid "The FEVER" – Listen to your spouse (coach)!

As I shared at the beginning of this book, I really wanted to purchase the new Honda Odyssey when it first came out. It was in the early days of DVDs, and this van was equipped with a DVD player integrated into its sound system. Amazing!

We had recently welcomed our first child into the family. Jenn and I had made a deal that when we had our second child, we would purchase a mini-van. Since we were hoping for a second child to arrive a couple of years after our firstborn, I started looking into purchasing a mini-van.

I caught a horrible case of car fever. I began to feverishly work the numbers in our "budget." This was more than three years before we really learned how to budget, and this "budget" certainly did not meet the INCOME – OUTGO = EXACTLY ZERO™ principle!

I plugged the huge payment for a new car into our budget. My car fever was so bad that I ignored the large financial issue created by this new bill. The shortage in our annual budget would have been more than $10,000. Instead of immediately eliminating the ridiculous car payment, I focused on reducing small costs like cable TV and other items which did not even remotely come close to balancing the budget.

Even though our budget was upside down by thousands of dollars, I remained determined to find a way to purchase the new vehicle. How would I have been forced to accommodate the negative balance created in our budget? Additional debt!

All I can say is, "Thank God for an awesome wife!" Jenn took one look at the budget and said, "Cut out the car payment!" When I did, the budget suddenly had a chance of becoming EZ™.

What I am really trying to say is that there will be times you will "get the fever" to purchase something. It may be a car. It may be a house. It may be land. It may be something else. When you put it on paper and work together with your spouse or financial coach, the chance of making a poor financial decision is greatly reduced.

Budget every single month.

Every single month is different. One month is full of weddings while another is full of Christmas. Summer requires travel, and fall arrives with expenses such as school tuition, clothes and books. At the end of each month, invest twenty minutes to review the calendar and plan your spending on paper. This allows you to review your financial performance over the past month and plan money decisions for the upcoming one.

You should prepare a budget every month instead of weekly, quarterly or annually because most of your ongoing expenses will happen monthly. This is usually the most appropriate time frame for financial planning. An annual budget can be helpful to gain an overall perspective of your finances, but a monthly budget will help you maximize every single dollar you receive.

Jenn and I were broke until we began to budget monthly. I had attempted budgets prior to December 2002. Notice that I said, "I." Jenn was not involved in the finances by my own choice, not her choice. The plans I had prepared were always annual budgets and were not broken down into monthly units. As a result, I had a budget that was not practical for monthly use.

Jenn and I had less than $1,000 in our savings account until we began to budget monthly. In fact, our savings account averaged more like $4.13. We spent every available dollar and utilized our credit cards to live beyond our means. As a result, we had no savings cushion, and we were digging a deeper hole in debt.

We finally learned the first rule of holes: "When you are in one, stop digging!" Once we started spending every single dollar on paper BEFORE we actually received the money and forced our budget to be EZ™, we began to win with our finances.

Follow the budget!

This seems obvious, but it is so hard to do this! Here is what usually happens when you commit to prepare and live by a written budget. As you finish preparing your first realistic budget, water will begin dripping from the ceiling onto the paper you just printed the budget on!

"Are you *really* committed to doing this?" the water leak will seem to ask. If you are not committed one hundred percent, you will find a reason to say budgeting does not work and abandon it.

You must follow the budget! What will happen when you need to repair a roof leak or replace a flat tire? Find a way to adjust the budget so you can make the repair without incurring debt. Certainly, it will be challenging, but you can do this! In fact, it is these very moments that will determine whether or not a person will truly be able to maximize their money and move toward a fully funded life.

What happens when you experience a flat tire? A ten dollar used tire will get you around until you can pay cash for a new one. When the engine dies on the car? Carpooling will work until it is repaired. As I write this book, I know of a person who lives in the country, but rides a bike to work to save money on gas. They are serious about transforming their financial future.

Sound crazy? Sound abnormal? It is! But it is because of this process that I am no longer broke. Prepare an EZ™ Budget every single month, before the month begins. Then make the courageous and challenging decision to follow it – no matter what. You will NEVER regret it!

Say "NO!" to yourself the 1st, 2nd, 5th, 82nd and 512th times you are tempted to break the budget.

Financial management is very similar to dieting. Just as dieters must still deal with food every day, you must handle money. The key is to establish a system that works for you and ensures you will stick to the plan. It is easy to tell yourself "NO!" the first and second times you are tempted, but what about the 56th time? What about the 125th time? Preparing and living by an EZ™ budget is what will allow you to win with your finances!

If you happen to fall off of the wagon, stand back up, dust off the budget, and get back after it. Living a fully funded life is worth the effort!

Teach your children about money.

I love public education. We have the best schools in the world, but they do not do the best job of teaching children how to handle their finances. They will not teach your children how to effectively manage money.

After I had completed twenty years of formal education, I had learned a lot about how to make money.

However, I learned very little about what to do with it once I earned it.

This is a key reason I wrote *What Everyone Should Know About Money Before They Enter The Real World,* a personal finance book for high school and college students. It is written with the goal of helping young people gain a positive start to their life and to help prevent common financial mistakes.

Can you imagine what your children will be able to accomplish if they learn key financial principles at a young age? Most can understand INCOME – OUTGO = EXACTLY ZERO™ by age six. By committing to teach your children financial principles, you will leave a legacy.

You can do this!

10 Savings

Saving money is crucial and essential to your climb up the IWBNIN Ladder. Without prioritizing savings, a fully funded life is virtually impossible to achieve.

In the hundreds of coaching sessions I have led, I am still amazed at people's lack of savings. It does not seem to matter how much money people earn, most still manage to spend it all – plus some more!

$20,000/year income – No savings!
$50,000/year income – No savings!
$100,000/year income – No savings!
$200,000/year income – No savings!

It is crazy! When reviewing surveys conducted during my live financial teaching events, it was shocking to discover that my young daughter had saved more money by the age of seven than the majority of the class.

Not shocking to you? Perhaps it will be more startling when I reveal that my daughter had $140 in her savings account when she was seven.

Most people have very little or no money saved. This makes me very sad. It makes me angry! It makes me yell, "What is going on? Why are we allowing ourselves to spend every single dime we receive and be snared in the horrible trap of having nothing left?"

It was this disturbing truth that compelled me to leave corporate America and begin a crusade to help others win with money! We simply MUST save money! This simple truth can be summed up this way:

"You can not prosper if you do not save."

Think of a wealthy person that you know. Now, think of wealthy person who does not have any money. It is impossible! Most wealthy people did not win the lottery. They built wealth by prioritizing saving and investing. A person cannot build sustainable wealth without prioritizing savings.

I choose to view savings as a debt I owe to my family. No one forces us to save. The government won't make me save. My children definitely don't help me save. The simple act of living life itself will continually challenge my ability to save. It is only my commitment to prioritize this important financial principle that ensures our family saves money.

The same is true for you. Your personal commitment is the only thing that will ensure saving money receives top priority in your monthly budget.

As Jenn and I have been preparing monthly budgets for years now, we have discovered there are three key reasons to save money.

Three Reasons To Save Money
1. Unknown, unexpected emergencies
2. Known, upcoming non-monthly expenses
3. Funding dreams

1. Unknown, Unexpected Emergencies

Life is going to happen. Someone will get sick. The car will break down. An appliance will fail. The roof will leak, but only when it rains. Unexpected bills will show up. Emergencies will happen – regardless of your financial situation. In fact, it seems as if these events occur more often when you have nothing saved!

If you do not have at least one month of expenses saved in an emergency fund (Rung #2 of the IWBNIN Ladder), you are at great risk of acquiring more debt. What will you do when the car breaks down? You will be forced to use debt to pay for the repair. What will you do when the kids have to go to the doctor? You will incur debt. The financial stress created by these events can be eliminated entirely by saving money.

Consider the following thought for a moment. Is it surprising that cars break down? Is it shocking that children will need new clothes? Is it stunning that Christmas is in December this year? Is it unexpected that you will have doctor bills in the future?

None of these items should be surprising. Yet, many times we are stunned when these events occur! Why do we experience such negative feelings and stress when faced with an unplanned financial challenge? Because there was no plan and nothing has been saved for so-called "emergencies." In reality, it becomes an "emergency" only because nothing has been saved.

I have learned to call things what they really are instead of what I hope or want them to be. Children growing and needing clothes, cars breaking down, roofs needing replaced, and medical bills – all of these sorts of events are going to happen. We do not always know which one will occur next, but we do know something will happen. And it will cost money. You can eliminate enormous amounts of stress by saving in advance for them!

This is why I encourage you to swiftly accomplish Rung #2 by saving at least one month of expenses. Of course, the more you save, the better position you will be in to face emergencies. Saved money provides a protective buffer around your life so you can absorb financial challenges without them completely derailing your life.

I regularly see an example in nature that demonstrates the need for a buffer. I live in South Carolina, and we have large man-made lakes built by the Army Corps of Engineers to collect water for use during droughts and to generate electrical power.

These lakes have no protection along their shores. When crazy people (like me) go to the lake and ski, we create large waves. These waves roll across the lake and smash full-strength into the shore. This results in severe erosion.

On the other hand, I have been to Minnesota many times for vacation. It is a state known as "The Land of 10,000 Lakes" because of its incredible amount of natural lakes.

People also ski up and down these natural lakes and send large waves crashing to shore. However, the impact on the shores of these natural lakes is vastly different. When a wave rolls in, lily pads start to weaken the wave. After encountering the lily pads, the wave encounters bulrushes which further weaken it. The result? The shoreline is greatly protected against erosion because of its naturally occurring shield against waves.

LESSON: *Natural lakes have natural built-in protection!*

Consider police officers and their bulletproof vests. Each weekend, we have police officers at our church to direct traffic. Even though they are at a church, each officer wears a bulletproof vest. Do you think they really believe they are in danger of being shot while at a church? Probably not, but they wear a bulletproof vest just in case.

On a blazing hot summer day, I'm sure the bulletproof vest is hot and uncomfortable. Why don't they just wear the bulletproof vest on the day they are going to get shot?

Just asking the question sounds silly. Every police officer knows they cannot predict the day when someone may shoot at them!

LESSON: *Police officers wear a bulletproof vest EVERY SINGLE DAY!*

As I am writing this book, a member of our church who is a police officer was investigating a robbery in progress. He was shot at least four times. His arm took two bullets and his bulletproof vest took the other two. I am glad he was wearing the vest. So is he!

For my friends who work in the manufacturing industry, here is another example that will help teach this principle of maintaining a savings buffer.

In my former life as an engineer and business manager for a manufacturing company, we had a particular customer who ordered product in a completely unpredictable manner. At times, they would order 50,000 parts. Even though they could not consume 50,000 parts in six months, they would place their order and demand next day delivery.

This customer was a large automotive manufacturer, and it was virtually impossible to change their ordering method. Our ability to gain future business depended on our ability to meet these short-notice orders.

It would take more than two weeks for us to produce this order, but the customer wanted them within

24 hours of order placement. If we had no parts saved up, this wild ordering pattern would prevent the most efficient use of our manufacturing team and equipment. To ensure we were always able to meet this customer's needs, we kept 75,000 completed parts in inventory. This saved buffer of inventory allowed us to absorb their orders without creating any chaos within our manufacturing facility.

We were able to do this because we had a plan, prepared appropriately, and maintained inventory.

LESSON: *Businesses carry inventory to protect themselves!*

So if we know that:
- Natural lakes have natural barriers
- Police officers wear bulletproof vests
- Businesses carry inventory

If we see these examples all around us, why on earth would we manage our life without the protection of an emergency fund? Every single wave that life sends your way will erode your ability to win financially. It will cause you to constantly change the way you manage money. This is what I call "letting your money manage you."

By accomplishing Rung #2, you will be able to absorb a financial emergency and continue on with life. As you achieve Rung #5 and achieve three months of expenses in your savings account, you will be positioned for long-term financial success. Through good planning, you can pay for emergencies as they happen without incurring debt or financial stress. This is what I call "managing your money."

If you do not have an emergency buffer fund, every problem you have will be accompanied by a money problem. Car problem? Money problem. Washing machine breaks? Money problem. By establishing an emergency buffer fund, you will just have a broken car or washing machine problem. The money part is taken care of!

One additional note to husbands: By establishing an emergency buffer fund, you will be enabling your wife to live a lower-stress life. She needs to know money has been saved to absorb the waves life sends your way. It represents security, and this matters a lot to my bride.

Because of our past money mistakes, Jenn has required our family to have an extra-large emergency fund. While my spending nature wants so badly to use the money, I leave it alone because I know how much stress and agony it prevents from happening in my life. IT IS SO WORTH IT!

2. Known, Upcoming Non-monthly Expenses (KUE)

When Jenn and I first started budgeting, we had another word for known, upcoming non-monthly expenses: BUDGET-BUSTERS! These expenses blew up our budget because they seemed to appear at the last minute, and we had not saved for them.

After experiencing a month where we had encountered a huge budget-busting expense, I always felt like the snake that swallowed an entire antelope. I would walk around rather stunned saying, "I can't believe I ate that whole expense this month." Because we had to eliminate other budget items to accommodate this "surprise" expense, I would then say, "I sure wish we had some money left for groceries!"

A few months after we began preparing a monthly budget, it became very clear that we must find a better way to pay for these KUEs. Through trial and error, we've solved the issue by implementing the following process. I'm confident it will help you too!

The first step is to recognize all of the non-monthly expenses that you know must be paid for in the future. Here is a list of common KUEs:

- Real Estate Property Taxes – Semi-annual payments
- Life Insurance – Annual premium
- Auto Insurance – Quarterly or annual premiums
- Car Repairs & Maintenance – As needed
- Health Club – Annual fee
- Golf Club – Annual dues
- Professional Organization – Annual dues
- Vacations – Whenever
- Income Taxes – Quarterly estimated or annual payments
- Christmas – Annually
- College Expenses – Future
- Car Replacement - Future
- Furniture Replacement - Future

The list could literally go on and on. The point is that these items are KNOWN and UPCOMING non-monthly expenses. A property tax bill should not be a surprise. No matter how much Christmas season creeps up on people, it shouldn't be a surprise.

Saving for these types of expenses is not a very difficult process. This is the good news. The real test is whether or not you will choose to implement it.

The Key: Accommodate your non-monthly expenses by saving for them every paycheck, or at least every month.

Suppose a person who is paid monthly plans to spend $1,000 for Christmas this year. In January, they could begin saving $83.33 each paycheck for the rest of the year. By December, they would have $1,000 saved for Christmas!

Christmas Example:

$$\frac{\$1,000}{Christmas} \div \frac{12}{Months} = \$83.33 / Month$$

Do you see it? Saving for KUEs will make your monthly budget more challenging, but it is far better than attempting to handle a massive expense all in one month. This realization was sufficient enough to motivate me to save *every* paycheck for these expenses.

Another way to look at this is to understand the escrow account for your house payment. For those who have an escrow account, there is never a concern about being able to pay for the property taxes or homeowner's insurance. This is because the mortgage company converts the annual cost of the taxes and insurance into a monthly charge and collects it as part of each month's payment.

Create an escrow account for your KUEs. It makes paying for these larger expenses so much easier!

Here's an example. Suppose David is paid a set salary every two weeks, and he needs to save money for the following KUEs over the next year:

- Vacation: $1,200
- Car Repairs: $1,200
- Christmas: $1,200
- Health Club: $720
- Property Taxes: $600
- Special Days: $500
- Life Insurance: $360
- Car Insurance: $960

To ensure these KUEs do not destroy his finances, David decides to save for them on a consistent basis. He utilizes the free Known Upcoming Expenses Calculator located in the "Tools" section of www.IWBNIN.com to determine the amount he needs to save out of each paycheck.

Known Upcoming Expenses Calculator

Pay Periods Per Year:	26

Non-Monthly Expense	Annual Expense	Per Paycheck
Vacation	1,200	46
Car Repairs	1,200	46
Christmas	1,200	46
Health Club	720	28
Property Taxes	600	23
Special Days	500	19
Life Insurance	360	14
Car Insurance	960	37
Total	6,740	259

He simply types in each expense, and the calculator does the rest. If David wants to prevent KUEs from destroying his monthly budget, he needs to save $259 per paycheck. Saving this $259 every single pay period will certainly be challenging, but it will be far less painful than attempting to pay for Christmas, a car repair, and property taxes all in one month!

You can easily calculate the amount you need to save each paycheck by using the "Known Upcoming Expenses Calculator" located in the "Tools" area of www.IWBNIN.com. If you prefer to calculate your KUEs by hand, a worksheet is provided for you here in this book.

Once you have calculated your "Savings Per Paycheck," I encourage you to make it automatic by establishing an automatic transfer from your bill paying account to a savings account. Set it to automatically occur every time you receive a paycheck. It took my family about three months to fully adjust our budget to accommodate the KUEs. After that, it became just part of the way we manage our money.

This process is how we experienced our first ever "cash paid for in advance" vacation in 2004. By automating our savings for summer vacation (a big KUE), we were able to pay cash in advance. It was amazing to experience a vacation *knowing* we had the money to pay for all of it and rejoicing in the fact that zero debt was being incurred. We've paid cash for every KUE since. So can you!

Known Upcoming Expenses Calculator

Non-Monthly Expense	Annual Expense	
Total:		1. Add up all KUEs
Paychecks Per Year:		2. Find your number below
Savings Per Paycheck:		3. Divide "Total" by "Paychecks Per Year"

Paychecks Per Year (use in above calculator):

- Once a month: 12
- Twice a month: 24
- Every two weeks: 26
- Every week: 52

3. Funding Dreams

Funding our dreams is the entire reason Jenn and I strive to manage money well. We have dreams we want to accomplish. So do you! We all have dreams. What dreams did you write down earlier? How much will it cost to fund each one of them?

I don't know about you, but I get no inherent joy out of paying my power bill on time. I know I should pay it on time and I do like electricity, but it just doesn't fire me up. What fires me up is being able to realize a dream!

In 2002, Jenn and I dreamed of moving back to Anderson, South Carolina to once again be an active part of a church we had helped start. We had the dream of helping our congregation learn how to manage money using biblical principles so they could fund their own individual God-given dreams.

To go on staff at the church, we knew it would require a major pay cut. After four years of focused effort, we funded our dream and moved back to Anderson. Even with the pay cut, we still smile about the decision because it was never about how much money we could earn – it was about funding a dream and living a fully funded life!

I want you to be able to achieve your dreams. I want you to be able to do EXACTLY what you have been put on earth to do. Even more, I know you can do it!

The sad truth is if someone continues to be mired in debt and does not save money, they are at great risk of never accomplishing their dreams. Dreams cost money, sometimes lots of money.

What are your dreams? What are you doing to accomplish your dreams? Earlier in this book, I challenged you to write down your dreams, and I really hope you took some time to do that. Now I encourage you to place a cost next to each dream and set a target completion date.

FUNDING MY DREAMS

DREAM	TARGET DATE	COST
	TOTAL COST	

SAVINGS

It's okay if the total cost of your dreams scares you. This is why they are called dreams. These financial tools will make it possible for you to accomplish them. The IWBNIN Ladder will help you climb to places you've only dreamed about.

It has happened for me. It can happen for you.

You can do this!

11 Debt Freedom

Debt – What should you do?

Eliminate it! The 8th wonder of the world, compound interest, will work against you every single day you pay interest to someone else! Interest payments have the power to keep you broke. I have yet to hear a person who is living a fully funded life tell me that their car loans and credit cards were the reasons they became wealthy.

If you have debt, what should you do? Start by calculating your Debt Freedom Date (DFD) using the Debt Freedom Date Calculator located in the "Tools" section of www.IWBNIN.com.

Begin by documenting every debt you owe. You will need to know the name of the debt, the balance owed, and the minimum monthly payment.

As an example, let's assume Tom and Mary owe the following debts.

	Balance Owed	**Monthly Payment**
Car Loan	$5,500	$378
Credit Card	$7,400	$125
Student Loan	$11,500	$135
Total Debt	$24,400	$638

Since Tom and Mary have committed to acquire no new debt, their DFD can be calculated by viewing these obligations as just one big debt ($24,400) with one big monthly payment ($638).

	Balance Owed	**Monthly Payment**
Total Debt	$24,400	$638

By dividing their $24,400 debt by their overall total monthly payments of $638, the calculator reveals a DFD of 38.2 months.

What if Tom and Mary found a way to eliminate $200 in expenses in their monthly budget? This extra money can be added to their monthly debt payments to achieve debt freedom more swiftly. The extra $200 toward debt each month increases their monthly payments from $638 to $838. Their new DFD is 29.1 months – nine months sooner!

$24,400 Balance Owed ÷ $838 Monthly Payments = 29.1 months

An astute person might object to this calculation saying, "You did not include the effects of interest."

This is a great observation because interest charges absolutely impact debt elimination. However, after teaching this principle to hundreds of thousands of people, I have been amazed to see that the average person who attacks their debt actually accomplishes it within the time frame calculated – or sooner!

Our team has actually conducted research to document the steps people have taken to speed up their climb to debt freedom (Rungs #4 and #7). Here are eight steps people have taken to accomplish debt freedom:
1. *Reduce interest rates* Many people with substantial consumer debt do not realize that 50% to 75% of their payments are merely going to the lender as interest – greatly reducing their ability to lower their debt. If you have high interest rate credit card balances, consider transferring them to a 0% interest balance transfer

credit card. Is your mortgage interest rate higher than those listed at BankRate.com? If so, consider refinancing the mortgage. It is amazing what a few hours of focus on interest rate reduction can do to speed up your DFD!

2. *Pay Raise* Are you being compensated fairly? Check out Salary.com for current pay rates of positions similar to yours. Take some moments to document how you are adding substantial value to your organization. If it makes sense to have a conversation with your leader, do it! Few things speed up debt elimination more than receiving additional income from your current job.

3. *Tax Refund* A tax refund might be an "interest free loan to the government," but it also represents an opportunity to force yourself to save money which can be used to impact debt in a big way.

4. *Bonus* A bonus can also be used to eliminate debt. Once you achieve debt freedom, it allows future bonuses to be used to fund dreams instead of paying for things from the past.

5. *Found Money From Better Budgeting* When I started preparing and living by a budget, it literally transformed my finances. I freed up hundreds of dollars each month that was disappearing in the form of "miscellaneous ATM cash withdrawals" and impulsive purchases.

6. *Sell Some Possessions* Sell the boat, motorcycle, extra car, and collectibles. Eliminating possessions will free up space, eliminate stress, and greatly speed up your climb on the IWBNIN Ladder.

7. *Work Overtime* If you have the chance to earn additional income by working extra hours, you can use this money to speed up debt reduction. Plus, the extra work

will mean you'll be too tired to spend the extra income frivolously.

8. *Extra Job* If you don't have the opportunity to work overtime at your existing job, obtain a second job – or start a small side business. The key here is to focus on something that is short term. You don't want to sign up for a permanent second job. Instead, commit to applying all additional money toward your debt. Your reward when you achieve debt freedom is being able to quit the extra job and prosper with only one job because you've freed up all of the money that was previously committed to payments.

The bottom line is this: The average person I coach using the Debt Freedom Date Calculator who is firmly committed to achieve debt freedom, usually accomplishes it in two-thirds of the calculated time – even though the calculation does not include the effects of interest!

One way to really speed up debt freedom is to sell a financed item – like a vehicle! Let's follow Tom and Mary's debt freedom journey.

Sell the car.

Tom and Mary actually have two cars, but one of them still has a payment. Every month, they send a payment of $378 to the car finance company. The vehicle is worth $6,000, but the loan balance is $5,500. They could sell the vehicle and completely pay off the loan. An additional $500 would remain after paying off the loan. They could save this money along with the next two month's payments they were scheduled to make ($378/month x 2 months = $756). This would provide them with $1,256 to purchase a special clunker that will get from them from point A to point B.

With the car payments eliminated, they could choose to continue paying the car payments – only now they could pay the payments to themselves! They could save $378 every single month. After six months, they would have $2,268 in savings! They could sell the clunker for $1,000, and put this money with their savings of $2,268 to buy a better vehicle. A $3,000 car should last for quite a while. They can now save up the $378 over the next twelve months. That would be $4,536!

If Tom and Mary were determined to become extremely strange (and not broke anymore!), they could choose to have only one vehicle. This decision would certainly require changes to their daily routine, but they want out of debt! By living with one car, they could free up the $500 in equity on the vehicle and save the $378 monthly payment PLUS the ongoing taxes, license plates, insurance, repairs, and maintenance that would have been needed for the car. Their savings over one year would look like this:

Item	Amount
Car Equity ($6,000 sell price - $5,500 loan)	$500
Car Payments ($378 x 12 months)	$4,536
Car Insurance	$400
Car Taxes, License Plates	$100
Maintenance/Repairs	$400
TOTAL	$5,936

In one year, Tom and Mary could save $5,936 just by making one courageous decision! In turn, they could use this money to speed toward their debt freedom date.

Their calculation would now look like this:

	Balance Owed	Monthly Payment
Car Loan	-	-
Credit Card	$7,400	$125
Student Loan	$11,500	$135
Freed up money from better budgeting		$200
Freed up money from car payment		$378
Freed up money from maintaining the car		$33
Freed up money from car insurance		$33
Freed up money from car taxes/license plates		$8
Equity from the sell of the car	-$500	-
TOTAL	$18,400	$912

Their debt freedom date calculation is now:

Balance Owed/Monthly Payment = $18,400/$912 = 20.2 months

If Tom and Mary sell their car, they will be debt free in just twenty months! They will have then freed up $912 EVERY SINGLE MONTH that no longer has to go back out to debt!

How much money do you pay EVERY SINGLE MONTH to make payments on your debt? Wouldn't you rather be able to save, spend or give away that money instead of sending it to a bank?

Pay an extra $838. Every $838 buys you one month!

As we learned, if Tom and Mary decide to keep the car, but they manage to spend $200 less every single budget, they will have $838 a month to attack their debt.

	Balance Owed	Monthly Payment
Car Loan	$5,500	$378
Credit Card	$7,400	$125
Student Loan	$11,500	$135
Freed up money from budget		$200
TOTAL	$24,400	$838

Balance Owed/Monthly Payment = $24,400/$838 = 29.1 months!

Tom and Mary may not be happy with 29.1 months. They want to become debt-free sooner. They have decided not to sell their car and are looking for other ways to achieve debt freedom sooner. In becomes apparent that every extra $838 they scrape together can be applied toward their debt and move their debt freedom date forward by one month.

This is when it gets really fun! Let's say Tom and Mary have just received a $2,000 tax refund. They could use $1,676 (2 months of $838 total payments) to move their debt freedom date two months closer!

Debt	Monthly PMT	Months
$24,400	$838	29.1
$24,400 - $1,676 = 22,724	$838	27.1

Jenn and I had so much fun with this as we eliminated our debt. Every time we encountered some extra money, we looked at the potential of moving up our debt freedom date.

For example, we looked into how soon we would become debt-free if we stopped contributing to my 401(k) retirement savings plan. By ceasing these investments, our debt-freedom date would have moved from 14 months to 10 months. However, investing enough in our company retirement plan to obtain the full company match (Rung #3) was the step before attacking our debt. While it would have been awesome to achieve debt freedom four months sooner, we stuck to our plan and continued the investment contributions so we could continue receiving the free company match to our retirement plan.

The key here is we made a decision. It was our choice. We thought through it, and discussed our options. We ran the numbers. In the end, it was just not worth stopping the investments and losing the company match (free money) just to become debt free four months sooner.

It is incredibly empowering when you work together to make money decisions instead of feeling like your money is out of control.

The Debt Snowball

There are two general debt reduction strategies offered by financial coaches. One strategy is to focus on debts with the highest interest rates first. The other strategy is to focus on the smallest balance owed first. This strategy is called the Debt Snowball.

Jenn and I chose to apply the Debt Snowball method. While both methods will work, I highly recommend this one because you will see individual debt payments disappear more swiftly from your monthly budget! When I was able to stop making payments to my credit card company, my progress was clearly noticeable!

Here are the steps you can take to apply the Debt Snowball technique to your debt.

1. Restructure high interest debt to lower interest rates
2. List your debts from the smallest amount owed to the largest
3. Pay minimum payments on all debts – except the smallest amount owed
4. Apply all additional money to the smallest debt
5. When the smallest debt is eliminated, take the monthly payment you were paying for that debt and add it to the monthly payment you are making on the smallest remaining debt.
6. Continue this process with intense focus until you are DEBT FREE!

Debt Snowball Example

Debt Name	Balance	Monthly Payment	
Doctor 2	320	50	A person has $23,205 in debt with a total of $640 in monthly payments. The calculated Debt Freedom Date is 36.3 months.
Doctor 1	685	50	
Hospital	1,300	50	
Furniture	2,400	75	
Car	5,000	140	
Credit Card 1	6,000	160	
Credit Card 2	7,500	115	
TOTAL	23,205	640	
Months Until Debt Freedom!	**36.3**		

After **6.4 Months** - Paid off "Doctor 2"!			
Debt Name	Balance	Monthly Payment	The $50 payment that was going to "Doctor 2" is added to the "Doctor 1" payment. Now "Doctor 1" will receive $100/month.
Doctor 2	PAID	OFF!	
Doctor 1	365	100	
Hospital	980	50	
Furniture	1,920	75	
Car	4,104	140	
Credit Card 1	4,976	160	
Credit Card 2	6,764	115	
TOTAL	19,109	640	

After **10.0 Months** - Paid off "Doctor 1"!			
Debt Name	Balance	Monthly Payment	The $100 payment that was going to "Doctor 1" is added to the "Hospital" payment. Now "Hospital" will receive $150/month.
Doctor 2	PAID	OFF!	
Doctor 1	PAID	OFF!	
Hospital	798	150	
Furniture	1,646	75	
Car	3,593	140	
Credit Card 1	4,392	160	
Credit Card 2	6,344	115	
TOTAL	16,773	640	

After **15.4 Months** - Paid off "Hospital"!			
Debt Name	Balance	Monthly Payment	The $150 payment that was going to "Hospital" is added to the "Furniture" payment. Now "Furniture" will receive $225/month.
Doctor 2	PAID	OFF!	
Doctor 1	PAID	OFF!	
Hospital	PAID	OFF!	
Furniture	1,248	225	
Car	2,849	140	
Credit Card 1	3,541	160	
Credit Card 2	5,733	115	
TOTAL	13,371	640	

After **20.9 Months** - Paid off "Furniture"!			The $225 payment that was going to "Furniture" is added to the "Car" payment. Now "Car" will receive $365/month.
Debt Name	**Balance**	**Monthly Payment**	
Doctor 2	PAID	OFF!	
Doctor 1	PAID	OFF!	
Hospital	PAID	OFF!	
Furniture	PAID	OFF!	
Car	2,072	365	
Credit Card 1	2,654	160	
Credit Card 2	5,095	115	
TOTAL	9,821	640	

After **26.6 Months** - Paid off "Car"!			The $365 payment that was going to "Car" is added to the "Credit Card 1" payment. Now "Credit Card 1" will receive $525/month.
Debt Name	**Balance**	**Monthly Payment**	
Doctor 2	PAID	OFF!	
Doctor 1	PAID	OFF!	
Hospital	PAID	OFF!	
Furniture	PAID	OFF!	
Car	PAID	OFF!	
Credit Card 1	1,746	525	
Credit Card 2	4,442	115	
TOTAL	6,188	640	

After **30.0 months** - Paid off "Credit Card 1"!			The $525 payment that was going to "Credit Card 1" is added to the "Credit Card 2" payment. Now "Credit Card 2" will receive $640/month.
Debt Name	**Balance**	**Monthly Payment**	
Doctor 2	PAID	OFF!	
Doctor 1	PAID	OFF!	
Hospital	PAID	OFF!	
Furniture	PAID	OFF!	
Car	PAID	OFF!	
Credit Card 1	PAID	OFF!	
Credit Card 2	4,060	640	
TOTAL	4,060	640	

After **36.3 months** - Paid off "Credit Card 2"!			DEBT FREEDOM!!! Now "YOU" will receive $640/month!!! AWESOME!!!!
Debt Name	**Balance**	**Monthly Payment**	
Doctor 2	PAID	OFF!	
Doctor 1	PAID	OFF!	
Hospital	PAID	OFF!	
Furniture	PAID	OFF!	
Car	PAID	OFF!	
Credit Card 1	PAID	OFF!	
Credit Card 2	PAID	OFF!	
TOTAL	0	640	

You can complete your own Debt Freedom Date Calculation by visiting the "Tools" section of www.IWBNIN.com.

Ben's Pickle Jar

My friend, Ben, decided he was going to become debt-free. At the time, he was a single father raising a daughter. As he began to ponder ways to achieve debt freedom, he realized he might have something of value that could really enable him to achieve debt freedom sooner.

Ben had a habit of buying crummy food items from the vending machines where he worked. Egg salad sandwiches (maybe made from ostrich eggs?), ham sandwiches (wild boar?), and miscellaneous unidentified items were all within the realm of possibility when he made a purchase from the vending machine. Poor taste in food notwithstanding, Ben had made it his habit of purchasing this food with a $5 bill and placing the remaining change into his pocket. Later in the day, having survived his first visit to the vending machine, he would make another purchase – with another $5 bill. The change would join the money from his earlier purchase in his pocket. At the end of the day, he would put the change in a jar at home.

One day while in a passing conversation, Ben mentioned that he likes to count change while watching football games. I asked him how much change he had, and he responded with, "Do you know those big pickle jars?" He made motions signaling the size of a large wholesale pickle jar one might purchase at a big warehouse store like Costco or Sam's Club.

"Yes," I replied.

118

"Well, I have one of those full of dollar coins," Ben said.

I nearly fell out of my chair! Do you know how much money that is?

For the next three days, Ben carried coins into the bank assuring them that he had not stolen them from a vending machine. After counting all of this money, he discovered his coins totaled enough to pay off his remaining debts and became debt-free!

Now, you may not have a pickle jar full of one-dollar coins, but I guarantee you have something valuable you could sell and speed up your climb to Rung #4 and accomplish debt freedom!

Look around your home. What could you sell? A bicycle? A piece of furniture? A TV? Movies? Art? A boat? A car? You have something. I know you do!

Ask yourself this question: "Is this item worth remaining in debt?" Sometimes the answer is "yes," but I've discovered that the answer is usually, "Absolutely not. Let's sell it!"

No more debt!

Remember, none of this will work if you continue to obtain debt. The calculation for debt freedom only works if you are no longer signing the line for more.

I have had broke people tell me they can't sell their cars (with debt equal to an entire year's salary) because they do not want their spouse to drive around in an unsafe car. Give me a break! A person who says this is exhibiting the behavior of a spoiled child. It is merely an excuse to continue poor financial decisions and avoid reality. The real reason a person is okay with crushing their budget with huge debt payments is because they are okay with living up to their eyeballs in debt. They are willing to put their financial future and relationships at risk over vehicles that will have hardly any value ten years from now.

I am through with bad debt that prevents me from living a fully funded life. Never again!

Do not skip rungs on the IWBNIN Ladder

You might be getting fired up to attack your debt while reading this chapter. This is a good thing! However, please remember that attacking debt begins on Rung #4 – *after* setting goals, saving money, and initiating your long-term investments.

As I mentioned in the IWBNIN Ladder chapter, the number one money mistake made by people is attempting to skip Rungs #1 through #3. While I fully understand the emotional energy we feel as it relates to eliminating debt, it will end up being unsustainable because life will happen. The life event will cost money. And if you've skipped the rungs focused on saving money, you will fall from the ladder and experience pain and agony as you incur new debt to pay for the life event. Follow the ordered steps up the IWBNIN Ladder, and you will have a safer trip toward achieving sustainable debt freedom and a fully funded life.

Make a decision today to eliminate debt. Calculate your Debt Freedom Date, with and without the home mortgage. Then challenge yourself to beat the goal dates you have established for each rung of the IWBNIN Ladder.

You can do this!

12 Investing & Compound Interest

Investing

COMPOUND INTEREST

$100/month for 39 years = $1,000,000!

$250/month for 31 years = $1,000,000!

$500/month for 26 years = $1,000,000!

$1,000/month for 20 years = $1,000,000!

Do I have your attention? This is real. Let me introduce you to the 8th wonder of the world: **Compound Interest**. It has the ability to completely change your life!

Investing is any activity which allows you to capture the power of compound interest and use it for your financial benefit. The following example demonstrates how this financial principle helps provide a solid foundation for your climb up the IWBNIN Ladder.

Suppose you have no money in your investment accounts, but you have recently arrived at Rung #3. You make the decision to begin investing $100 each month. You establish an automatic draft from your bank account into an investment account to ensure this investment happens every month.

In this example, I am assuming your investment choices will deliver an increase of 12% per year (1% per month). In the first month, you invest $100.

Year	Month	Principal	Interest	Contribution	Final Value	Invested
1	1	0	0	100.00	100.00	100.00

In the second month, $100 is invested for the entire month. If it increases in value by 1% each month, your investment will grow by $1.00 ($100 x 1% = $1). At the same time, an additional $100 is automatically transferred from your bank account into your investment. This will bring the total value of your investment to $201 ($100 from previous month + $1 increase in value + $100 additional investment this month).

Year	Month	Principal	Interest	Contribution	Final Value	Invested
1	2	100.00	1.00	100.00	201.00	200.00

The third month is where the POWER of compound interest begins to appear – even if it is in a small way! The $201 remains invested for the entire month. The $1 you gained last month will also earn money for you. Your investment will grow $2.01 ($201 x 1% = $2.01). The $1.00 you earned last month earned $0.01 for you this month! Isn't that amazing?

Year	Month	Principal	Interest	Contribution	Final Value	Invested
1	3	201.00	2.01	100.00	303.01	300.00

It may seem silly to celebrate earning a penny, but I am FIRED UP because I already know what this will look like when you have $100,000 invested! By continuing to invest $100 each month and achieving 12% annual growth, your investment will reach $100,000 in just 20 years and 2 months!

Year	Month	Principal	Interest	Contribution	Final Value	Invested
20	2	100,015	1,000	100.00	101,115	24,200

In 20 years and 2 months, you will have $100,015 even though you will have contributed only $24,200 (242 months x $100/month = $24,200). Your account will have gained a total of $75,915 in interest! Amazing, isn't it?

Remember, back in month three, it was $1.00 that gained you $0.01. Now, the $75,915 interest earned will provide $759.15 IN ONE MONTH ($75,915 x 1% = $759.15). The money you personally invested over the previous 20 years and 1 month will gain you $241.00 this month ($24,100 x 1% = $241). This means your total gain in this month is $1,000!

Now, with all of this math, I'm sure you feel like you have accidentally gone back to a horrible high school algebra class. You may be tempted to check out on me (or burn this book). Please do not do it! I beg and plead with you to continue reading this chapter. All you must know right now is that you need to make it your habit to invest money every single month. To eliminate the drudgery of the math exercises, let me just show you what $100/month at 12% annual growth looks like in five year increments.

$100/month investment (12% annual growth)

Time	Value	Time	Value
5 years	8,167	30 years	349,496
10 years	23,004	35 years	643,096
15 years	49,958	40 years	1,176,477
20 years	98,926	45 years	2,145,469
25 years	187,885	50 years	3,905,834

This is with an investment of only $100 per month. After 40 years, you will have invested $48,000 of your own money (480 months x $100/month = $48,000), but your account will have grown to $1,176,477. Of that huge amount, $1,128,477 is interest. Behold the power of compound interest!

Compound interest can work against you.

Any loan requiring you to pay interest is an example of compound interest working against you. A common example of this is a home mortgage.

Let's say you have a 30-year fixed rate home mortgage balance of $100,000 at 6% interest. If you pay it off in exactly thirty years with identical monthly payments, how much interest will you have paid the bank for that $100,000 loan?

**Mortgage Paid: $100,000   Interest Paid: $115,838
Total Paid: $215,838**

This is not a typo. You will have paid a bank $115,838 in *interest* for the $100,000 mortgage loan. It will require total payments of $215,838 just to eliminate the $100,000 loan. EXPENSIVE!

This is the reason a bank's name is usually on the nicest, biggest building in town. Like any business, they have a goal to make your money become their money. Thirty-year mortgages are just one excellent tool they use to accomplish their goal.

By choosing to pay additional money toward the principal each month to pay off the $100,000 mortgage in just 15 years, you would pay a total of $151,895 for the $100,000 loan. You will eliminate $63,943 in interest paid PLUS you will be the outright owner of your home 15 years *sooner*!

An "Early Pay-Off Calculator" is located in the "Tools" section of www.IWBNIN.com. It can be utilized to determine the impact that additional principal payments will have on debt elimination.

This is exactly what I did in 2006 for the home my family purchased when we returned to Anderson, South Carolina. Using the "Early Pay-Off Calculator," I adjusted the payment amounts to different levels. For fun, I gave each of the varying payments a name. One was the "we can do this with no problems" payment. Another was a "we can do this but we will feel some financial stress" payment. Still another was an "our finances will enter into a nuclear winter if we pay this amount each month" payment. We settled on something in the middle, and ended up paying off our 30-year mortgage in just 6 years.

What a celebration we had when our bank's website read "PD OFF." They couldn't even bring themselves to spell out the word "PAID" in its entirety. I jokingly say, "I would like to buy two vowels, please." And with the house payment gone, we could certainly afford the vowels.

Do you see how compound interest, if not addressed, can work against you in a big-time way? Any loan which requires you to pay interest transforms wonderful compound interest into a force that works against you.

Financing a new car is another example of compound interest working against you. Even if you receive zero percent financing.

Let me explain. The new car will decrease in value nearly 60% over the next four years because it is a depreciating asset. A new $25,000 vehicle will be worth only $10,000 five years later even if you did "pay" 0% interest. Where did the other $15,000 go? Into thin air. Behold the power of compound interest working against you!

Retirement – How much will you need?

This is a key question many people never think about for longer than sixty seconds. Usually, this question is accompanied with overwhelming feelings that can cause a person to ignore the situation. But it is a fair question. How much will you need to retire? The answer begins by determining the amount you would like to receive from your investments during each year of retirement. If you make $50,000 a year, are you expecting to also have $50,000 a year in retirement? More? Less?

Once you've decided the amount you would like for each year of retirement, a relatively simple calculation can provide a solid goal for the amount you should strive to save. This calculation is explained in the next few paragraphs. However, if you are part of the majority of people who really don't like math, you will be glad to know that a free "Retirement Nest-Egg Required Calculator" is located in the "Tools" section of www.IWBNIN.com.

For the calculation, you need two numbers – (1) the amount of money you want to use each year and (2) the annual rate at which your account will be growing.

$$\frac{\text{Amount For Each Year}}{\text{Annual Growth Rate of Investment}} = \text{Nest Egg Required}$$

For example, if you would like to continue to have $50,000 a year and expect your investment to grow 8% each year during retirement, the Retirement Nest-Egg Required calculator shows you will need $625,000 in retirement savings on the day you retire.

$$\frac{\text{Amount For Each Year}}{\text{Annual Growth Rate of Investment}} = \frac{\$50,000}{8\%} = \$625,000$$

126

If you have $625,000 in your retirement account and it grows 8% annually, you will earn $50,000. This allows you to spend $50,000 and maintain a retirement account balance of $625,000!

Now, inflation is an economic reality that reduces the value of your money each year. It is the reason a 15¢ candy bar thirty years ago now costs at least four times as much and is half the size it used to be.

Inflation has averaged between 3% - 4% for several years. To keep up with 4% inflation, you will need to give your nest egg and annual spending a 4% cost-of-living raise each year. If you plan on spending $50,000/year and you expect to earn 8% on your account AND you want to give yourself a cost-of-living raise every year, you will need to use the following equation.

$$\frac{\text{Amount For Each Year}}{\text{Annual Growth Rate of Investment - Annual Inflation Rate}} = \frac{\$50,000}{8\% - 4\%} = \$1,250,000$$

If you have $1,250,000 in your retirement account growing at 8% annually, you will gain $100,000 each year. To give your account a cost-of-living raise each year, you will also need to keep 4% of each year's growth in the account. In the first year of retirement, the 4% equals $50,000. You could spend $50,000 of the $100,000 gained while leaving the other $50,000 in the retirement account. This means you will now have $1,300,000 working in your investments to produce next year's spending money and cost-of-living raise!

In summary, three key figures will help determine how much money you need to save to ensure a fully funded retirement:

1. *Amount Wanted For Each Year of Retirement* This is money above and beyond any guaranteed retirement money you will be receiving during retirement such as Social Security, military retirement, and defined pension benefits. The more you want to spend each year, the more you will need to have accumulated in your investment account on the day you retire.

2. *Annual Growth Rate of Investment* This can be wildly different from person to person. One person may continue to take substantial investment risk throughout retirement while another may choose guaranteed growth rates. The higher the growth rate achieved, the less you will need in your investment account when you retire.

3. *Annual Inflation Rate* You can't predict inflation, and nothing can account for it when it runs rampant. The higher the inflation rate, the more you will need in your investment account when you retire.

Assuming a 12% investment growth rate at 4% inflation, you would need to save $625,000 (instead of the $1,250,000 at 8% annual growth rate) to enable a withdrawal of $50,000 per year.

$$\frac{\text{Amount For Each Year}}{\text{Annual Growth Rate of Investment - Annual Inflation Rate}} = \frac{\$50,000}{12\% - 4\%} = \$625,000$$

How much money will you need to have saved at retirement? Look at the provided chart to see the amount you would need to have saved in order to retire today.

Assumes 12% Annual Growth Rate of Investment			
Assumes 4% Annual Growth Rate of Inflation			
Amount For Each Year	Nest Egg Required	Amount For Each Year	Nest Egg Required
20,000	250,000	90,000	1,125,000
25,000	312,500	95,000	1,187,500
30,000	375,000	100,000	1,250,000
35,000	437,500	105,000	1,312,500
40,000	500,000	110,000	1,375,000
45,000	562,500	115,000	1,437,500
50,000	625,000	120,000	1,500,000
55,000	687,500	125,000	1,562,500
60,000	750,000	130,000	1,625,000
65,000	812,500	135,000	1,687,500
70,000	875,000	140,000	1,750,000
75,000	937,500	145,000	1,812,500
80,000	1,000,000	150,000	1,875,000
85,000	1,062,500	155,000	1,937,500

Did you find your number? What feelings are you experiencing right now? Are you on track for a great retirement – a fully funded retirement?

If you have $143 saved up and are 53 years old, it is high time to get started. If you are 20 years old, time is on your side. Start your investment journey immediately!

How do you begin investing for retirement?

A frequent question I am asked is, "How do I start?" It is a great question! Let me first review the options most people have available to them.

Self-Directed Retirement Saving Plans at Work

The number one way people invest today is through self-directed retirement saving plans (RSP). If you are an employee of a for-profit business, your company probably offers a 401(k) plan or similar RSP. Non-profit organizations often offer similar plans such as 403(b) and SIMPLE IRAs. These plans allow you to invest money into a variety of market-based investments, each with a different level of risk and reward. A key feature of self-directed retirement plans is the option of contributing portions of your paycheck prior to taxation. This tax advantage provides substantial incentive to participate in the plan offered by your employer.

For example, you can invest $100 a month into your 401(k) (Rung #3), but your take-home pay will not be reduced by the entire $100. Government rules allow you to redirect the tax dollars you would have paid to the government and instead place them into your retirement account. You will be required to pay taxes once you begin withdrawing the money during retirement, but you will be able to use the tax dollars to help earn interest all the way up to your retirement. The chart below helps explain this.

Year	Month	Tax-Deferred Value ($100/mo)	Post-Tax Value ($70/mo)	Difference
5	60	8,167	5,717	2,450
10	120	23,004	16,103	6,901
15	180	49,958	34,971	14,987
20	240	98,926	69,248	29,678
25	300	187,885	131,519	56,365
30	360	349,496	244,647	104,849
35	420	643,096	450,167	192,929
40	480	1,176,477	823,534	352,943
45	540	2,145,469	1,501,829	643,641
50	600	3,905,834	2,734,084	1,171,750

At the end of five years, the difference is only $2,450. However, the point has been clearly made how very important it is to build up your retirement account as quickly as possible. Look at the difference after twenty years: $29,678. In year thirty: $104,849. If you have fifty years of saving in front of you, the difference of being able to utilize the tax dollars is $1,171,750!

Take the offer from Uncle Sam to utilize tax dollars for your investments. Your company's self-directed retirement plan is a great place to start.

In addition to the fact that you have the opportunity to invest your money prior to taxation, many employers will match at least a portion of your contributions. This is FREE MONEY! I once worked for an employer that provided a 100% match for retirement contributions for up to 8% of my pay. This was an unbelievable opportunity, and I took full advantage of it. Another employer matched 100% of my contributions up to 6% of my pay. Again, this company match is free money, and it is part of your compensation. This is why investing begins on Rung #3 of the IWBNIN Ladder. It is important to begin investing early – even more so when a company match is available.

Here is what is very alarming to me. At every company I have worked for, nearly half of the employees were not taking advantage of this free money. I had one question for those people – WHY?!!!

Terrible reasons were provided such as:

- "I can't afford to contribute."
- "I am living paycheck-to-paycheck already."
- "Our investment opportunities are terrible."

Let me be really clear on this. If a person chooses not to invest when a company match is available, they are really saying they are not able to afford having the company hand them FREE MONEY. Whenever I encounter people who have made this choice, I want to hand them a shirt that says, "I choose to be broke!" I simply don't understand it.

Here are some practical ways to start your investment journey:

1. RUN to your Benefits Department and ask how you can sign up for your company's retirement plan.
2. Start contributing something. At least contribute enough to accomplish Rung #3 by establishing an investment that will receive the maximum possible company match.
3. As quickly as possible, move your investment contribution to at least 15% of your gross income (Rung #6). Yes, I know this is a lot of money, but you will never regret this decision. People who contribute at least 15% of their gross income to their retirement savings plan for the majority of their working lifetime are the ones who retire wealthy.

A verse in the Bible, Proverbs 13:11, comes to mind: "He who gathers money little by little makes it grow."

What if my company does not have a self-directed retirement plan or doesn't match my contributions?

There are still many options available to you. This book does not include an exhaustive list, but the following options are some common ones available to most people.

Roth IRAs

This type of IRA allows you to invest money that has already been taxed – your take home pay. This money can be invested in the same variety of stocks, mutual funds, and other investments just like any other IRA, but the difference here is that it will grow completely free of taxes and will not be subject to taxation upon reaching retirement age.

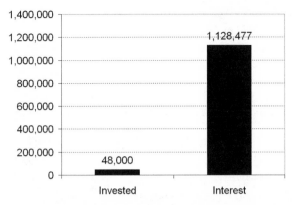

In our example of investing $100 each month for 40 years, which category was larger: The amount invested or the interest gained? If you invest $100 monthly for 40 years and it grows 12% annually, you've invested $48,000 but the interest is $1,128,477. The interest gained is by far the largest amount, and it is free of taxes in a Roth IRA!

A website dedicated to this type of IRA is located at www.rothira.com.

Traditional IRA

This is an IRA where you can invest before-tax money. The money can be invested in the same variety of stocks, mutual funds, and other options just like any other retirement plan. Because you have the advantage of using before-tax money, you will be taxed once you begin withdrawing money at retirement.

In most cases, you can begin investing with as little as $25 as long as you sign up for automated monthly drafts of at least $25 from your bank account. Many investment companies offer this option.

Real Estate

Your personal residence is another investment that grows in value tax-deferred and possibly tax-free!

Although there are income limitations, you are currently able to earn $250,000 ($500,000 if married) tax-free on the sale of your personal residence as long as you have lived in it as your primary residence for two of the past five years.

We have previously covered the need to pay off the house as soon as possible due to the fact that compound interest is working against you. The beautiful thing with a house is that it is real tangible property that helps diversify your investment portfolio. It also has the intangible qualities of pride of ownership and security.

I share many more investment alternatives and approaches in my book *Oxen: The Key To An Abundant Harvest*. As you prepare to prosper through investing, I encourage you to obtain a copy of this book. It is focused on helping people move from being an "average investor" to a "savvy and informed investor." It also has a self-study and video lessons available to help put your investment dreams into action. You can learn more about *Oxen* by visiting www.iwbnin.com and clicking on "Store."

Automate. Automate. Automate.

Make your investments automatic. Arrange your investments so money is put into the account every single month. I have arranged for money to be automatically drafted from my account each month for my company's Simple IRA (our organization's self-directed retirement plan) and to the 529 college savings plans for our children. I do not have to think about it, because it is automatic. It just happens. I never see the money, and it helps my net worth increase every single month!

I was reminded of the power of automating our investments when Jenn and I moved back to South Carolina in 2006. We had to change banks, and this meant we had to close the bank account from which our daughter's 529 college savings plan was auto-drafting. It took a few months to establish the automatic draft from the new bank account, which meant I had to manually write a check each month for our college fund investment. It was challenging. There were so many other ways I could have used the money. I genuinely believe that if I had to write a check every month to the college savings account or to my investment accounts, my investing plan would be seriously behind. Make your investments AUTOMATIC!

Start NOW!

The sooner you start, the less you need to save each month to reach your goals. If you begin investing $100 each month at age 25 and continue for the next 40 years, you could have $1,176,477 by age 65. If you wait until age 40 to start, you will have to invest $626 each month to achieve the same wealth by age 65. If you wait until age 50 to start, you must invest $2,354/month!

Let's state this another way. Suppose a person named Randy is 25 years old and begins investing $100 each month and continues to invest the same amount every month for the next ten years. In ten years, Randy ceases contributions – probably because he didn't read this book. Randy will have invested $12,000 by age 35. With 12% annual growth, his investment will be worth $826,986 upon retirement at age 65 – even though he did not contribute *anything* for the last 30 years!

Now let's say Randy's friend, Bob, is also 25 years old, but he wants to put off investing for ten years. After ten years, he starts investing $100 per month and does so every single month for the next thirty years. At age 65, Bob has personally invested $36,000 – $24,000 more than Randy. However, because Bob made the mistake of waiting ten years before beginning his investment, his investment is only worth $349,496 at age 65 – $477,490 less than Randy.

In fact, in the following chart, we see that Bob will never catch up with Randy.

Time	Randy	Bob
5 years	8,167	0
10 years	23,004	0
15 years	41,791	8,167
20 years	75,922	23,004
25 years	137,927	49,958
30 years	250,572	98,926
35 years	455,214	187,885
40 years	826,986	349,496
Total Invested	**12,000**	**36,000**

When it comes to investing, time is your friend. Start NOW!

Opportunity Cost

How much are you currently paying in debt payments each month?

For the average family, it is between $500 and $1,250 per month not including the home mortgage payment. What if you accomplished debt freedom (Rung #4) and no longer had to send this money to banks every single month? What else could you do with this money?

"What else could you do with this money?" This is the definition of Opportunity Cost. You can only use your money once to purchase something. Once the money is spent, it is gone. Whenever Jenn and I receive extra money, we always stop and ask ourselves the question, "What are the different opportunities we have to use this money?"

As I mentioned earlier in this book, when Jenn and I were focused intensely on becoming debt-free, we considered stopping our retirement contributions. We could have used this money to help speed up our debt elimination. However, when we looked at the big picture (knowing the power of compound interest, Proverbs 13:11, and other facts), this move would help us become debt-free only four months faster than if we kept contributing to the 401(k). Achieving debt-freedom four months sooner was simply not motivating enough for us to make this adjustment. Plus, we would have lost the 100 percent matching contribution from my employer.

The key here is that we looked at all of our different opportunities before spending the money. We chose the option that best suited our family. We looked at our options BEFORE making a choice. This allowed us to make the best decision for our money.

This process of always considering the opportunity cost is so powerful! Instead of feeling as if our money was managing us, we were managing it. What a novel concept! I love this because it is what has enabled my family to accomplish exactly what we have been put on this earth to do. And I know it can do the same for you and your family!

Investments go UP in value

I once heard someone say, "I invested in a new car for the family." The statement hit my ears in about the same way the sound of cat's claws on a chalkboard would – it drove me crazy!

Good investments go UP in value. A new car will drop WAY DOWN in value. It will lose most of its value within the first five years. It is certainly nice to own a new car, but it is definitely not a good investment. The goal is for your investments to go UP in value. Never forget this.

Summary of Investing

Why do you want to achieve financial freedom? I really hope you have accomplished Rung #1 by writing down your plans, hopes, and dreams. What exactly is it that you have been put on this earth to do? I really believe you have been created *on* purpose *for* a purpose.

However, every single dream you have will cost money. If you want to fund the biggest dreams of your life, you must invest. A farmer clearly understands this fact. What if the farmer chose to "hope" for a harvest but refused to sow seed into the ground? There would be nothing to gather at harvest time! The farmer would have a better chance of capturing a magical unicorn than he would of reaping an abundant harvest. It is with this thought that I sum up the principle of investing:

There is no HARVEST if you do not INVEST.

When you have a written plan for your life with specific hopes and dreams, it will drive you to manage your finances better. It is not going to just magically happen. It requires FOCUS-pocus, not hocus-pocus. It is critical that you prioritize investing. Establish your investments, make them automatic, review them regularly, and choose to win with your money!

You can do this!

13 Insurance

Insurance. I send so much money off each month to insurance companies that at times I wonder if it is worth it. Have you ever wondered the same?

Here are all of the types of personal insurance Jenn and I have:

- Term Life Insurance
- Homeowner's Insurance
- Auto Insurance
- Health & Dental Insurance
- Long-Term Disability Insurance

In this chapter, I am going to explain why I carry these types of insurance. This is definitely not a complete summary of all types of insurance. My goal is to explain the types of insurance Jenn and I own and share why we own them.

I am challenging you to be able to explain the reasons you own your insurance policies at the same level of detail. Many people are paying premiums on insurance policies they don't even need! A friend who sells insurance told them they needed it, so they signed up for it. Or a slick insurance agent used some big language and a horror story to confuse and scare them into purchasing a policy.

My budget felt substantially less financial pressure when I started asking questions about my insurance and truly understood the policies I possessed. Here are the magic words I used to save tons of money on insurance: "I need a better deal."

Level Premium Term Life Insurance

Jenn and I have thirty year level term life insurance. Suppose I have a thirty year $500,000 level term policy with a premium of $250 per year. Level premium means the annual insurance cost will remain the same ($250 per year). Term means the insurance will last for a specific period of time (30 years).

Term life insurance is very straightforward. If I die at any time within the insurance term (30 years, in this case), my beneficiaries will receive the full face value ($500,000) of the life insurance policy. If I do not die during this term, the insurance will expire without paying anything. I am personally rooting against dying in this thirty year period!

This form of life insurance is very cheap and easy to understand when compared to other life insurance products available. The primary reason I have purchased this insurance is to replace my income should I depart life earlier than expected. I carry an insurance policy equal to ten times my annual income. With an income of $50,000 per year, this would mean a person should obtain a $500,000 policy. If I pass away while my children are still in the household, I want Jenn to be able to focus on raising them without having to worry about replacing my income. Term life insurance allows me to know my income would be replaced.

For a healthy thirty-year-old male who doesn't use tobacco products, a $500,000 policy would cost about $25 a month. For a healthy thirty-year-old female, the same coverage would cost around $20 per month. That's really cheap for such great coverage.

140

The website, www.zanderins.com, is a great place to obtain term life insurance quotes. You can also obtain quotes from the "Next Steps" section of our website – www.iwbnin.com.

There are many other forms of life insurance available, but they are usually much more expensive when compared to term life insurance. Any type of life insurance is a bargain if you die prematurely and someone collects on it (not a bargain if you're the one dying!). I prefer, however, the most financially prudent method of protecting my family in the event of my untimely death. I am able to accomplish this with term life insurance.

My personal goal is to become self-insured. If you are able to become debt-free and invest wisely, you will eventually have enough money that your need for life insurance will diminish greatly. Think about it. Suppose you die, leaving behind no debts and more than a $1,000,000. You have probably become self-insured.

Life Insurance Tips
- Ensure you understand the policy you are buying
- Keep it simple
- Obtain an amount equivalent to ten times your annual income in term life insurance
- Pay annually as it is usually 10 to 30 percent cheaper!
- Obtain at least three quotes – one of them from an independent insurance agency
- Do not allow a gap in coverage
- Do not cancel an existing life insurance policy until you have a replacement life insurance policy in place
- Always ask for a better deal

- Use caution when purchasing insurance from a friend or family member since your judgment could become clouded
- Obtain life insurance of at least $250,000 for a stay-at-home spouse

Homeowner's Insurance

You are required to acquire homeowner's insurance by the mortgage loan company. Even when you have paid off your home, homeowner's insurance allows you to transfer risk for a small price relative to the home's value. Homeowner's insurance generally costs one percent or less of a home's value. For a $100,000 home, expect homeowner's insurance to cost $1,000 or less per year.

It is important to purchase guaranteed replacement value homeowner's insurance. Without guaranteed replacement value, you could still end up absorbing a major loss if the house were to be destroyed. For example, suppose a person had homeowner's insurance that covered $100,000 in rebuilding costs, but over time, the cost to rebuild increased to $125,000. If the house were to burn down, the homeowner could be liable for $25,000 of the reconstruction costs! By having a guaranteed replacement value policy, you will ensure your home and your wallet are fully protected.

If you are currently renting, be sure to obtain renter's insurance. The landlord does not carry insurance on your possessions. Their insurance covers only the dwelling. The renter is required to insure their personal items. Renter's insurance is very affordable and great way to transfer risk.

Homeowner's Insurance Tips
- Always have homeowner's insurance if you own a home – even if it is paid for

- Ensure you fully understand the product you are buying
- Obtain guaranteed replacement value insurance
- Ensure your home's contents are fully covered – especially valuable items
- If you have auto insurance or some other insurance, ask for a "bundle" discount
- Consider increasing the deductible to reduce your premium cost. If you are managing your money well and have built your emergency fund to at least three months of expenses (Rung #5), you may consider increasing the deductible. This can result in a substantially lower insurance premium.
  - o Example: If you increase your deductible from $500 to $1,000 and the premium drops by $400 a year, this is probably a no-brainer. The premium is the only cost guaranteed to happen, and an event requiring the use of the insurance is not. If you are able to make it fourteen months without a claim, you will come out ahead financially. Even if a claim happens two years down the road, you will pay the $500 more in deductible, but you will have saved $800 in premiums (two years at $400 per year in reduced premiums due to increasing the deductible by $500).
- Shop around for the best rates every two years
- Obtain a minimum of three quotes – one of them from an independent insurance agency

Auto Insurance

The first reason Jenn and I have auto insurance is because it is required by law. This is a pretty motivating factor!

It also allows us to transfer risk to the insurance company. Suppose I was involved in a two-car accident that totaled both vehicles. Let's say I was responsible for the accident. My car insurance policy provides me with the ability to replace both vehicles as well as pay for the medical bills. Doctor bills resulting from auto accidents can easily add up to tens of thousands of dollars.

When my family achieved Rung #5, we increased the deductible from $250 to $500 because the premium was $200 per year less. While we took an extra $250 of risk (the increase in deductible), we would save money overall if we were able to go fifteen months without causing an accident. See how it works?

	Lower Deductible ($250)		Higher Deductible ($500)	
Year	Premium	Deductible	Premium	Deductible
1	$1,000	$0	$800	$0
2	$1,000	$0	$800	$0
3 (accident)	$1,000	$250	$800	$500
Total	$3,000	$250	$2,400	$500
3 Year Total Cost	$3,250		$2,900	

Because the $200 savings was so good, I was willing to take the risk of having to pay for a higher deductible. However, if the premium reduction was only $20 per year for increasing my deductible by $250, it would not have been worth the risk. I would have to be accident-free for more than twelve years to come out ahead financially. Statistics and my driving capability tell me this probably will not happen!

Auto Insurance Tips

- Always have auto insurance
- Bundle with other types of insurance to get discounts
- Shop around for the best rates every two years
- Obtain at least three quotes – one of them from an independent insurance agency
- Obtain quotes with different deductibles
- Obey the traffic laws
- Be very cautious buying car insurance from family or friends without getting quotes from other places

Health Insurance

The cost of medical insurance is outrageous and has spiraled out of control. However, it must be a priority. Medical insurance costs huge amounts of money because medical bills are so high.

Which would you rather have happen when you experience a major illness or surgery? Pay medical insurance premiums and only owe the insurance deductible or have no insurance and end up owing $20,000, $50,000, or even $100,000 because you had no health insurance?

This is why I have chosen to pay for health insurance every month. Everyone in my family is covered. While it is very expensive, I clearly understand its importance because Jenn has had two major surgeries and I have had one. Each one cost more than $14,000. Two surgeries occurred within ten months of each other. If we would not have had medical insurance, I might not have ever been able to write a book titled, *I Was Broke. Now I'm Not.* I might have had to write, *I Was Broke. I Still Am.* No one would want to read that book!

Shop around for better deals. Make the decision to at least carry insurance that covers huge expenses – like a high deductible health insurance plan. This type of insurance requires you to pay a significant amount of medical expenses before the insurance will pay anything. After reaching the deductible, the plan will usually pay for the majority (if not all) of your additional health care costs for the remainder of the insurance year. This type of insurance is much cheaper than comprehensive care, but you should be financially okay if you have reached Rung #5 and have established a fully funded emergency fund of at least three months of expenses.

My medical insurance provider also negotiates rates with medical groups. As a result, I receive "discounts" on what the normal charge would be. I put quotes around "discounts" because it is hard to believe that a $1,000 charge per day for a hospital bed is a discounted rate.

Medical Insurance Tips
- Get over being irate at the cost and get covered – even a high deductible plan can seriously limit the costs you would pay in the event of a major medical event
- Shop around – usually your employer health plan will be better than what you can get on the open market as an individual, but it is still worth shopping around
- Make sure you clearly understand what the insurance will and will not pay for
- Have health insurance at all times as you never know when you are going to need it

146

Long-Term Disability Insurance (LTD)

If I were to become disabled and lose the ability to speak, write, or perform the duties of my work, I would also lose my ability to produce an income by working. Even though I would be disabled, life would still cost money. How would I be able to generate an income to pay for my ongoing expenses? LTD insurance helps me transfer this risk. Many employers provide this as it is usually relatively cheap for them to provide.

If I were to become disabled, LTD Insurance will pay 50 to 60 percent of my income until I am able to perform my duties again.

I prefer same-skill LTD insurance. This type of insurance will pay until I am able to return to my normal work. Suppose I were disabled because I lost my voice and was unable to fully recover my ability to speak and teach. Speaking is a large part of my crusade. As a result of losing my voice, I would not be able to do what I have been created to do. I want insurance that will pay if I am unable to do that type of work. I do not want insurance that will stop paying just because I am able to walk around again. In the insurance world, they call my preferred LTD policy "Own Occupation" insurance. The type I do NOT want is "Any Occupation."

Long-Term Disability Insurance Tips
- Ensure you clearly understand the policy
- Obtain this insurance – Don't allow a gap in coverage
- Make certain you obtain "Own Occupation"
- Ensure any LTD policy provided via your employer is portable – that it can be taken with you should you no longer be an employee of the company

Summary

These are the types of insurance policies Jenn and I possess and why we obtained them. Can you explain why you own each of your policies in the same detail?

Insurance Transfers Risk

Ultimately, insurance products were created to transfer risk. Life will happen, and there is nothing you can do to prevent it. Having the appropriate insurance is a foundational element that will help you remain on the IWBNIN Ladder without having a life event knock you completely off of it.

If you choose not to obtain insurance, you could be standing on Rung #9 living a fully funded life and then receive a cancer diagnosis. Without health insurance, surgery and a few rounds of chemotherapy will wipe out a lifetime of saving and investing.

If you think about it, your emergency fund is a form of insurance. When the engine fails on your car, you can use your savings to have it fixed. Your emergency fund protects you from incurring debt.

You can't protect against everything in life, but you can take several key steps to prevent most of them from destroying your finances. I encourage you to spend some time reviewing your insurance policies and ask yourself three questions:

1. Why do I have each of these insurance policies?
2. Am I receiving the best deal possible?
3. Do I need to acquire any new insurance policies?

It may not be the most exciting task you've ever done, but it will provide peace of mind and help your climb up the IWBNIN Ladder be a much smoother trip!

You can do this!

14 The Time Is Now!

I have been on my climb up the IWBNIN Ladder for many years now, and not one rung has been easy. There are many things that have attempted to distract me, but I've been blessed to be able to continue the climb and experience a fully funded life. During the journey, I've learned a few things that have helped me stick with my climb – even when I was tired, frustrated, or outright angry with my progress.

Keep Focused

From day one, I have kept my family's financial goals pinned on the wall where we pay our bills. It is a regular reminder of why we have chosen to take this journey. It provides the power and energy to stick with the plan.

When faced with unexpected health problems, we remained focused. When the doctor told us we couldn't have any more children, we remained focused. When we discovered we were pregnant without maternity insurance because the doctors told us we couldn't have any more children, we were overjoyed and remained focused throughout the financial challenge of paying cash for our baby boy. When we learned three years later that another baby was on the way (this time *with* maternity insurance – we learned our lesson!), we were able to welcome another beautiful baby girl to our home without losing focus. When we launched I Was Broke. Now I'm Not. as a business and made very little money in our first year, we remained steadfastly focused. When we purchased a company, INJOY Stewardship Solutions, we continued our focused financial efforts.

Since July 2003, we've never skipped a single month of preparing a budget. We prepare a budget each month for each of our businesses. Every single day. Every single month. Every single year.

Proverbs 21:5 shares "The plans of the diligent lead to profit, as surely as haste leads to poverty." I encourage you to remain diligent – focused – on employing the financial fundamentals. Remain steadfastly gripped to the IWBNIN Ladder. Use financial challenges as a moment to learn instead of giving up.

Financial Coaches

Without wise financial counsel in my life, there is no way I would have achieved my goals. When I was broke, I felt embarrassed about my situation and chose to hide the problems. When I stopped being prideful and sought out people who were winning with money, I began to prosper.

In sports, we see that great teams have great coaches. Even in individual sports, the winners all have coaches and mentors. If you want to win at the money game, you need some coaching. Our team has trained thousands of coaches all over America and Canada. Most of them provide coaching at little or no cost! If you are super serious about taking your finances to another level, I encourage you to check out the I Was Broke. Now I'm Not. Core Coaching Program (CCP) – a 12-month online training course I teach to equip people to master their finances. You can learn more at www.IWBNIN.com/ccp.

Community

I have discovered that it is much easier to win with money when my friends and family are also focused on climbing the IWBNIN Ladder. When we first started out, all of our friends were broke. We made a decision to start living by a budget, but our friends weren't on board. Consequently, they were continually asking us to go out to eat with them at restaurants. Our budget screamed loudly that we could not go out to eat, but it was very difficult to tell our friends that we could not join them. It became a lot easier when we helped them begin living on a budget too! We had a lot more meals together at each other's houses which was far cheaper and turned out to be an incredible way to build stronger relationships.

Long before *I Was Broke. Now I'm Not.* and its group study existed, Jenn and I began teaching classes at our church to help people begin winning with money. It built strong community as we all shared our experiences with money – both good and bad. If you are interested in helping a group of your friends win with their money, I encourage you to check out the *I Was Broke. Now I'm Not.* Group Study at www.IWBNIN.com. It will build community, and help you in your journey too!

Continual Learning

When I made the key decision to change my financial behavior so I could begin living a fully funded life, I was determined to gain financial wisdom. I began reading every personal finance book I could get my hands on. From Dave Ramsey to Robert Kiyosaki. From Mary Hunt to Howard Dayton. From David Chilton to David Bach. From Larry Burkett to Bishop T. D. Jakes.

I read the entire book of Proverbs in the Bible and was particularly struck by Proverbs 4:7 which shares this

151

golden nugget: "The beginning of wisdom is this: Get wisdom. Though it cost all you have, get understanding." What are you willing to *pay* to gain financial knowledge?

I have set up my Internet browser to open 68 different websites each time it opens. I have made it my habit to read them every single morning as I begin each day. Many of the sites are focused on personal finances, and they help me continually learn what is happening in the financial world.

Money and the management of it is constantly changing. A commitment to learning will help you be aware of those changes and allow you to prepare for them.

As the old statement says, "There are people that happen to things, and there are people who have things happen to them. Then there are people who wonder, 'What happened?'" Lifelong learners are people who will be able to "happen to things."

A Final Word

So there you have it. Everything you have just read outlines the exact steps Jenn and I have taken and the tools we have implemented to win with our money and make the days of having only $4.13 in our savings account a distant memory.

We have been able to accomplish far more than we ever thought possible – all because we said "NO!", "Wait!", and "Not now!" Because of our decision and commitment, we've been able to impact hundreds of thousands of people, but it won't be complete without YOU.

Your time has come. It is your turn. I can not manage your money for you. I have poured myself into this book and into providing free tools and lessons at www.IWBNIN.com. All with one goal in mind. The goal to equip you to win financially and live a fully funded life.

It is time for your to climb on up the IWBNIN Ladder and take your finances to another level – a place you've only dreamed of achieving. The world awaits you and your God-given dreams, talents, and abilities. Become debt-free and pursue those passions with 100 percent of your energy. I can't wait to hear what you accomplish – all because one day you decided to win with your finances!

As you begin to live your own fully funded life, I would like to ask one favor of you. Would you please carry this crusade to others? I need your help to take this to the nations! Give this book to a family member or friend. Help them put together their first-ever budget and debt freedom date calculation. Give them a boost onto the first rung and help them begin their climb up the IWBNIN Ladder. And as I'm sure you know by now, the tools to get them started are all available at www.IWBNIN.com.

You can do this!

I Was Broke. Now I'm Not.
Financial Freedom Experience

The Financial Freedom Experience is an online course geared to help you take your next step with your personal finances. Whether you need help with a budget and are living paycheck-to-paycheck or you're looking to invest for the future - this course has something for everyone!

It contains 10 life changing video coaching sessions delivered online and on-demand at your pace. Participants receive access to advanced financial teaching and tools. With this program, you can literally hire Joseph Sangl to be your financial coach.

= LEARN MORE & REGISTER =
www.IWBNIN.com/FFE

I Was Broke. Now I'm Not.
Small Group DVD Study

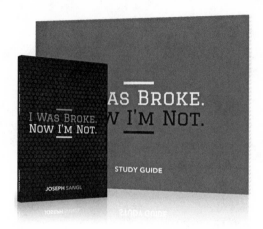

A six-week DVD-based personal finance study designed to complement *I Was Broke. Now I'm Not.* Each kit includes a copy of *I Was Broke. Now I'm Not.* and the accompanying Group Study Guide. Only one kit is needed per family. Be sure to pick up one Group Study Leader Kit as well to ensure that you have the DVD lessons!

= LEARN MORE & PURCHASE =
www.IWBNIN.com - "Store"

What Everyone Should Know About Money Before They Enter The Real World
Book + Group Study

A perfect resource for those just beginning their money journey! In this book, Joseph Sangl equips young people with practical principles and tools that will help them win with their money and avoid making major financial mistakes.

Topics include:
- Planning for life
- Budgeting
- Giving
- Saving
- Debt
- Student Loans
- Credit Scores
- Investing & Compound Interest
- Insurance
- Purchasing A Home

This is the PERFECT book for high school and college students!

= LEARN MORE & PURCHASE =
www.IWBNIN.com - "Store"

Oxen: The Key To An Abundant Harvest

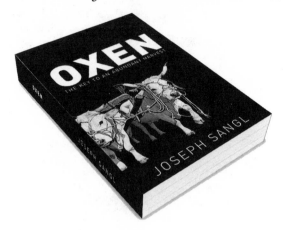

You have huge hopes and dreams for your life. Unfortunately, most of them will cost so much that they may appear almost unachievable. If you are doing everything possible to win with your money, but feel like you are spinning your wheels financially, this is the book for you.

In *Oxen* Joseph Sangl shares principles that will help you maximize your financial resources, so you can experience an abundant harvest and fund your biggest dreams. You will learn how to:

- Leverage the power of oxen
- Identify and acquire oxen
- Earn income even while you are not working
- Measure and build net worth
- Fund your dreams

Oxen is not a theory. It is timeless truth that has been applied by millions to achieve an abundant financial harvest. Your dreams are huge. They can be funded. *Oxen* will help you do it.

= LEARN MORE & PURCHASE =
www.IWBNIN.com - "Store"